Power Through Purpose

The Realism of Idealism as a Basis for Foreign Policy

Power
Through Purpose

*The Realism of Idealism
as a Basis for Foreign Policy*

---

by THOMAS I. COOK *and* MALCOLM MOOS

Baltimore, The Johns Hopkins Press

Distributed in Great Britain
by Geoffrey Cumberlege: Oxford University Press

Printed in the U.S.A.

Library of Congress Catalog Card Number 54-11253

☆ TO Katherine AND Tracy

Preface

The United States is the heir and standard-bearer of a culture begotten and bred in Europe. That culture rests on the twin foundations of Graeco-Roman politics and law and Judaeo-Christian ethics and religion. Our own tradition and history give us a unique position as modern champions of those ancient insights. Our constitutional democracy and our industrial technology provide us with unique opportunities to realize the Western promise in the daily practice of our lives and through the sure functioning of free institutions. We are equipped to achieve both citizenship as social and political participation in the shaping of our lives and destinies and the full development of the ultimate and irreducible person. Possessed of vast power and called to leadership in the world, we can, if we will, spread our ideals elsewhere and help others on the road to their realization. Our middle-class society is marked by an increasingly shared amplitude of economic means and by broad enjoyment of leisure for the cultivation of humane ends. It is the true classless society, without benefit of revolution or need for totalitarian discipline. It is the leader in the fight against these needless and soul-destroying ills, and against their spread. Its mission is to persuade those still free that they can with its help profitably and successfully follow its way, and to rescue those who are the victims of tyranny and set them, too, on the right path. To that end it must first strengthen its adherence to its own ideals and institutions at home, and purify its political practice. It must fight without compromise the internal enemies of its method of freedom. It must maintain without compromise the essential rights of those committed to those methods, and must champion the values of creative dissent and personal difference. Its foreign policy must no less clearly and forthrightly distinguish between friend and foe, and must be devised as an integral part of the total politics of a nation whose interest is international and whose ethical principles rightly claim universal validity.

Such are the theses of this book. In propounding them, the authors have sought to clarify the issues in the present "Great Debate," and to fight the extremes of utopian worldism and realistic nationalism.

Acknowledgments

Acknowledgments for stimulus, aid and comfort in the genesis and execution of this work must necessarily be divided. Its immediate cause was a long review by Moos of Hans Morgenthau's *In Defense of the National Interest*. A discussion of this review with Cook revealed a like-mindedness on, and common concern with, the issues involved. At the suggestion of Moos, Cook re-shaped and expanded the review into an article.

The enterprise and collaboration grew. Two preliminary statements, entitled respectively "Foreign Policy: The Realism of Idealism," and "The American Idea of International Interest," appeared in the *American Political Science Review* for June, 1952 and March, 1953; while Chapter 3 of this book, in essentially the same form, was published by the *Journal of Politics*, to whom the usual thanks are due, in February, 1953.

But the real genesis of the work, which brought together an ex-Englishman trained at the London School of Economics, and then at Columbia, and a mid-Western Republican who sprang from Minnesota, goes deeper.

The senior author, who received initial stimulus to an interest in international affairs from Philip Noel-Baker in England and the late Parker T. Moon at Columbia, discovered a real concern to develop a relevant theory of international relations and foreign policy in conversations with his good friend Linden Mander, sometime Australian, at the University of Washington. Those conversations were resumed, with a different person but the same atmosphere and orientation, when he came to The Johns Hopkins. While the collaboration was in progress, two events gave added stimulus, promoted insight, and produced rectifications of viewpoint. First, he went as a substitute for his colleague, and through the latter's kindness, to a conference at Asheville, North Carolina, arranged by the Brookings Institution under the auspices of the late Leo Pasvolsky. There he learned much from discussion with Southern colleagues, a brilliant group of officers from the Armed Forces, and select persons from various government departments who had special competence in areas of foreign policy. Secondly, thanks to the interest of Captain J. C. Wylie, well met there, he was subsequently able to spend several days at Newport discussing policy issues with the Advanced Class at the Naval War College. That select company constituted the most extraordinary seminar of able and mature men he has ever encountered. Moreover, by demonstration of ability rather than by any deliberate attempt, they were promoters of profound lay confidence in the custodians of our security.

To various classes and seminars at Hopkins which listened with attentive interest to readings of selected sections of the manuscript, and to members thereof who offered perceptive criticisms and flattering encouragement, he owes thanks; as also to colleagues who discussed and debated various points, sometimes unaware of his own design or the collaborative project.

Finally, he wishes to record a deep debt of gratitude to his wife, Katherine Dane Cook, who listened willingly through seemingly endless false starts, drafts, and revisions, however inconvenient the occasion; and creatively criticized both style and substance.

The junior author has little to add to his colleague's very generous comments on the genesis of this volume. Cook has, of course, been its chief architect, and Moos is indebted to him for a shared intellectual experience that has brought together the resources of a political theorist with those of a political behaviorist in what they trust has yielded some light on the compelling issue of the hour—American foreign policy. To the several people acknowledged by Cook for assistance, Moos likewise adds his own thanks and dares to venture the hope that this modest undertaking will aid in further clarifying what the late Senator Vandenberg termed "The Great Debate."

Both authors wish here to signalize their deep gratitude for work, editorial as well as secretarial, on this, as on many another manuscript, by Mrs. Edna L. Fulton, whose careful and constructive interest in all the productions of members of the Department of Political Science at The Hopkins is hidden under the deceptively simple title, secretary.

They wish, too, to offer public thanks to numerous colleagues throughout the country who, aware of their enterprise through the aforementioned articles or otherwise, have encouraged them in their labors and endorsed their general viewpoint with an emphatic "go to it, and more power to you." Nor are they unmindful of their debt to that lesser band who have expressed reservations, and even scepticism, and have offered general or specific criticisms from which they hope they have been able to profit. Likewise, they have gained much from a noble company of writers on foreign policy whose views are in varied degree opposed to their own. Indeed, without such goading, and particularly that contained in the writings of Professor Hans Morgenthau, this book would never have been written. To the smaller company of their precursors who are in this area intellectual allies they offer homage for pioneering, and hope that they have here done no disservice to a common cause. Nevertheless, while they make the usual and obvious statement of sole responsibility, they wish at the same time to insist that they have at best merely synthesized and systematized views they know to be widely held today, though hitherto not fully expressed.

Contents

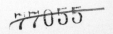

Power Through Purpose

The Realism of Idealism as a Basis for Foreign Policy

I

The setting
for American policy

Bipolar conflict of purposes

The principal problems of American foreign policy arise from the sustained tension between the United States and the Soviet Union. Each has its supporters, though in the one case they are allies; in the other, satellites. Each competes for the support—moral, material, and military— of uncommitted peoples. Each has profound interests and seeks by persuasion and power to extend and secure them. Those interests appear to be incompatible and irreconcilable. For each power represents a radically different form of government. Each embodies a radically different concept of culture. Each takes a radically different attitude towards the nature of international law and organization. Each espouses a radically different doctrine of obligation toward other peoples and governments. Hence the conflict, being between two antithetical ways of life and thought, is genuinely bipolar.

Nevertheless, each of the chief adversaries professes a profound desire for peace and assures the world that it has no intention of provoking war against the other. Yet, each accuses the other of attitudes and behavior incompatible with such protestations of peaceful intent. Each is fearful and suspicious of the other. Each is righteously indignant at the other's actions and arguments. Each is self-righteous and proclaims its own correctness without reservation. Each therefore doubts the assurances given the world by the other. Hence each feels insecure. For each is convinced that the other's assurances are merely propaganda to gain support and constitute weapons in a cold war whose purpose is either to prepare for a hot one or to gain victory over the other without battles.

What is more, each is, in a sense, right. For this major conflict of our day is a civil war within Western civilization. It is, moreover, a struggle to determine which power shall be the bearer to the East of the blessings and promise of the West. It is, that is to say, a battle as to which of these great subcontinental states is the proper leader and standardbearer of industrial technology and of that democracy which is its requisite complement. It is, more profoundly, a struggle as to which side truly embodies the Western activist heritage; which correctly interprets its ethical insights, liberty, equality, and justice; which provides the proper path to secure the conditions of human fulfillment. Finally, from the Western viewpoint, the conflict is a crusade against a dangerous heresy begotten within Western culture itself.

Doubts as to the likelihood of peaceful settlement are therefore justified. So, too, are suspicions that the opposing camps desire peace only on condition of total victory for their respective interpretations. Furthermore, the Western world can properly accept an accommodation with the U.S.S.R. only if and when the latter abandons and repents its fundamental heresy and ceases to promote its erroneous views as to human destiny and the path for its pursuit.

A brief initial statement of the stands of the parties should make the profound depth of the conflict clear. According to Marxist-Leninist teaching, capitalist nations must inevitably wage war. They are driven thereto by the contradictions inherent in capitalism and by its consequent crises. All capitalist societies are retrogressive and unable peacefully to escape cyclical depressions and unemployment. War and war economies offer temporary relief, however much they lastingly weaken the system. Because they are helplessly declining, capitalist nations must and do desperately seize on this palliative. It is, nevertheless, their ultimate doom. For it creates conditions for revolution within them, as today it may give opportunity for Communist powers to intervene forcefully and give the *coup de grâce*.

Unfortunately, however, the Soviet Communist argues, capitalist aggressive war today will be directed against Communist countries. In the past, wars were between capitalist nations. They were the civil wars of the capitalist system. The proletariat suffered as cannon fodder. But the disciplined Communist leadership could still regard such wars as hastening the day of Communist triumph. Further, it could prepare to grasp the psychological and sociological moment to attain victory by revolutionary seizure of power. Today the capitalist powers do not indulge in such palliative internecine strife. They grimly seek to destroy Communist nations, and above all the U.S.S.R., before it is too late. For otherwise the conspicuous successes of Communism in creating a better and richer order, and the manifest contrast of declining capitalist powers, which are unable to solve their economic and social problems, will in due course bring revolution in the latter and the ultimate world triumph of the former.

Communist peoples, their propagandists insist, desire only peace, so that they may develop fully the resources of their lands, enjoy an ever-increasing well-being, and attain a brilliant culture in which all men shall share. But the capitalist world, properly fearful of Communist demonstration of how good life can be for ordinary men, cannot permit such peace. It has to attack and must make its objective the total elimination of Communist institutions, for it cannot confront a genuinely just, equal, and free society. Such a society by example renders capitalist ethical professions manifest hypocrisy in the defense of unjust privilege and exploitation.

The Communist theorists therefore contend that mere prudence, not less than obligation to their own theory and practice of genuine social justice, requires that Communist nations prepare for self-defense. For they will be forced to fight; by the nature of the situation capitalist powers cannot be sincere in their professed desire for peace. What is more, the Communist peoples, hounded into war, must be ready to destroy the aggressors. They must put an end forever to their evil designs and to their institutions, at once antiquated and oppressive. Then men will at last be freed and capable of effective pursuit of happiness. Such an intention, however, is not aggressive; the Soviet world would cheerfully live in peace and allow time and inherent internal contradictions to destroy capitalist governments and classes. From solicitude for its own peoples and for the oppressed in capitalist countries, it would indeed vastly prefer such a course, confident that the outcome was not in doubt.

Such is the Communist thesis, as currently expounded by Russian and Chinese leaders and thinkers. The Western viewpoint lacks a like coherence—the consequence of neat dogma. Its essential themes may nevertheless be briefly indicated. In essence, the response of the West, and especially of the United States, is that capitalism in the Communist sense is nonexistent. The Communist interpretation is a myth and a dangerous delusion. For it is totally unrelated to the course and practice of Western industrial and democratic society. The real inequalities and injustices perceived by Marx a century and more ago have not grown greater and worse with the passage of time. On the contrary, the so-called middle class has vastly increased in numbers. At the same time labor, and especially organized labor, has achieved rates of pay which compare favorably with those of white-collar workers. Progressive taxation has meanwhile lessened the gap between rich and poor. Its proceeds have been used in considerable part to improve the conditions of workers and farmers and to increase their security. Mass production and distribution have made available to most men rich and varied goods and have rendered them inexpensive. The health and the life expectancy of the population as a whole has risen.

Simultaneously, class differentials in their enjoyment, once so conspicuous, have slowly but surely decreased and continue to do so. Technology and industrial management have reduced backbreaking drudgery and monotony. The hours men spend at work have lost much of their past misery and have, in an increasing number of instances, become a source of satisfaction. Thanks to high level production and to the efforts of trade unions, most men now enjoy considerable leisure. Public and private provision have, moreover, made possible most varied uses of leisure time, with consequent satisfaction for all sorts and conditions of men. With America in the lead, Western society has in varying degrees combined democratic political institutions, guarantees of personal and group rights, and industrial technology. It thereby has secured increasingly and peacefully the blessings of a genuinely classless society, wherein diverse personalities gain the fulfillments of free men without conflict and without compulsion.

On these grounds, the non-Marxist insists that the descendants of Marx have been blinded by their doctrine. They have not observed, they cannot see, they will not look at, the vast, rich, and satisfying social panorama stretched before their eyes by and in the West. Driven by dogma, they magnify flaws and imperfections out of all proportion. They fail utterly to note progressive improvements and falsely deny the sustained and conscious search for betterment. As a consequence, they cannot perceive the irrelevance and error of their teaching that nations they persist in calling capitalist must go to war. The democratic and industrial West, aware of its achievements, actually knows no such crises as the Communists depict. It feels, rather, that it has at last successfully eliminated the shocks of extreme trade-cycle fluctuations. Convinced of its superiority in achievement and that its path is progress and promise, it desires peace. It finds the necessity of war industries and defense measures a wretched frustration and an exasperating delay in its meliorative course. Such undertakings are thrust upon it by the doctrines of its opponents—by their consequent policies of vast armament, expansion, and subversive activities which they have directed to frustrate merely imagined Western designs and to promote pointless revolutions. Left in peace, as it desires, the West is confident that it can achieve the real goods promised by the Communists for the classless society, as indeed it has in many areas achieved them already. It can likewise avoid, as those who follow its way may avoid, the violation and corruption of liberties and the resultant perversion of the very ends that are also professedly pursued by its chief opponent. Western analysts are driven to conclude that the teachings sponsored by the Soviet Union are an expression of envy and of resentful inferiority. Its practices appear deliberately calculated to hinder Western achievement of the good life and to lessen the present gap between the two groups by the enforced necessities of Western defense.

Moreover, the Western observer is forced by the propaganda of modern Russia to the conviction that some form of Soviet satellitized confederation of nations is the ultimate objective of the Communist heirs of Marx. The Westerner perceives that the cold war technique is simply a crass perversion of Spinoza's "Peace is not merely the absence of war" for the purpose of winning a Sovietized peace without war. Changes in the party line within the Soviet Union reinforce his belief that defeat and overthrow of powers not Communist after the Soviet pattern, and under Russian leadership, is the sole and uncreative objective of the rulers of the U.S.S.R. They not only insist that capitalism must be destroyed; they regard independent communist dictatorships as traitors to the supposed duty to destiny and right, as Soviet diatribes against Tito's regime in Yugoslavia make clear. The observer concludes that Russian blindness to actual Western achievement is deliberate. The professed concern of the party leaders and theorists for the universal attainment of human well-being involves much hypocrisy in addition to delusive dogma. The whole movement aims at a world order under Russian direction.

The initial errors of Marxist teaching have, then, been compounded (even as that teaching has been progressively perverted) in the service of Russia's traditional nationalistic and imperial ambition, now magnified beyond all proportion. Testimony to this development may indeed be found in the divergent definitions of "cosmopolitan" in the 1935 and the 1948 editions of the official Soviet Encyclopedia, which indeed make sense only on such an interpretation. In 1935, a cosmopolitan was "one who asserts he belongs to no single nationality, but regards the whole world as his home." By 1949 he had become "a person of anti-patriotic, bourgeois opinions who asserts hypocritically that the whole world is a single fatherland and who refuses to defend his own country." This last definition, it is vital to realize, occurred long after the German invasion had been repelled and at a time when Russia had successfully used its position in the United Nations to minimize the possibilities of effective international co-operation on a world-wide scale.

The two powers

Present bipolar conflict rests, it is true, on fundamental differences in ethics and in ideology. But it is also a conflict between the Soviet Union and her satellites, on the one hand, and the nations of Western Europe, North and South America, on the other. In that conflict, it is Russia which aims at indirect, if not direct, world domination. For it is Russia, inspired by Marxist teaching, which denies the possibilities of peaceful coexistence of different social-economic orders; denies the claims of effective diversity in ways of looking at and ways of doing things; denies that nations may be united in their efforts to better their own and other peoples unless and until they all accept one doctrine and one discipline.

Nevertheless, the actual polarization of political power is not due solely to the teachings of Marx as adapted to international relations by Lenin and twisted in the service of Russian interests by Stalin—whose overall policy Malenkov apparently intends to continue, with whatever expedient and temporary modifications. The process has proceeded quietly for well over a century, as the new challengers for leadership in the world, America and Russia, have edged their way into the top tier of world powers, and the former leaders, the Great Powers of Western Europe, have declined. With exceptional foresight, Alexis de Tocqueville wrote in 1835:

There are, at the present time, two great nations in the world, which seem to tend towards the same end, although they started from different points; I allude to the Russians and the Americans. Both of them have grown up unnoticed; and while the attention of mankind was directed elsewhere, they have suddenly assumed a most prominent place among the nations; and the world learned their existence and their greatness at almost the same time.

All other nations seem to have nearly reached their natural limits, and only to be charged with the maintenance of their power: but these are still in the act of growth; all others are stopped, or continue to advance with extreme difficulty; these are proceeding with ease and with celerity along a path to which the human eye can assign no term. The American struggles against the natural obstacles which oppose him; the adversaries of the Russian are men: the former combats the wilderness and savage life; the latter, civilization with all its weapons and its arts; the conquests of the one are therefore gained by the plowshare; those of the other, by the sword. The Anglo-American relies upon personal interest to accomplish his ends, and gives free scope to the unguided exertions and common sense of the citizens; the Russian centres all the authority of society in a single arm: the principle instrument of the former is freedom; of the latter, servitude. Their starting-point is different, and their courses are not the same; yet each of them seems to be marked out by the will of Heaven to sway the destinies of half the globe.[1]

Tocqueville's prophecy was remarkable indeed; and it required the changes of a century to give meaning and content to what was then the imaginative vision of a seer. In Tocqueville's day, Jacksonian America was agrarian and mercantile. It faced inward, across its own continent. Its industry was little developed, and that little was located chiefly in New England and the East. The railroad age had just begun. The Mississippi was still a major artery of commerce and the chief road to the West. Men still traveled slowly; mobility was limited; and social and cultural life was largely local. Tocqueville perceived American restlessness and American ingenuity, just as he appreciated our political participation, individual courage and energy, and the creative powers of voluntary groups and local communities. Together these constituted the seed and core of democratic promise. But Tocqueville could hardly foresee the vast growth of American industry, the industrial cities of the Middle West, and the recent dispersion of factories in the Far West and the South. He could hardly foresee the modern

---

[1] Tocqueville, Alexis de, *Democracy in America,* Henry Reeve, trans. (4th ed., New York: Henry G. Langley, 1845), I, p. 470–71.

tempo of technological change, the magnitude and constant impact of organized research, the deliberate invention of invention. He could hardly foresee megalopolis and suburbia; the access of city workers to rural charms and leisure pursuits, and the ready accessibility of town and city amenities to those who live and work on farms. He could hardly foresee the mobility of men in the age of automobiles and trailers. He could hardly foresee the easy mass distribution of goods by vast transcontinental freight trains and by an endless chain of trucks which thunder over arterial highways and serve small and inaccessible towns on country roads. He could hardly foresee the transport of goods and men, for peace or war, across all the continents and oceans by huge planes nor envisage the speed and global range of modern communications both for peace and war. He could hardly foresee America as the great exemplar of gigantic engineering projects which controlled nature to enrich man, and as the most extraordinary depository of individual and collective technological skills. Yet it is these developments which have given her that position of world leadership which Tocqueville envisioned as her destiny. These have made her the promise of that democratic way of life which he perceived to be—with all its possible dangers and defects—her great contribution to human betterment, her moral appeal, and her expanding destiny.

In some respects, Tocqueville's awareness of Russian destiny was even more remarkable, as his perception of the nature of its political order and power is today doubly impressive in the light of the liquidating of its Revolution. For he lacked that firsthand familiarity with Russia which he possessed of the United States. He wrote no analysis of that country comparable to the magnificent *Democracy in America*. The Russia of his day had abandoned alike the weird vision of a Holy Alliance urged by Alexander I and the practical participation in Western European affairs which had marked the heyday of the Concert of Europe. Russia was for the moment turning inwards. It was fearfully committed to unreforming reaction and to suppressing the national ambitions of subject peoples. In government a monarchical despotism of limited efficiency, it was socially a limited aristocracy based on ownership of land, on imperial favor, and on office-holding. Its economic system was feudal and agrarian, supplemented by town trade and handicraft industry in the service of court, aristocracy, army, and bureaucracy. Its native and nomadic peoples were, in the main, ignored. Its vastnesses were partly unexplored, largely unsettled, and hardly exploited at all. Its communications were backward and totally inadequate to efficient administration. Western doctrines of progress, which had penetrated or had been imported earlier, were not in the ascendant; and those who shared them were largely driven to ineffective opposition or futile protest. Apart from a small professional class, some merchants, priests in the Orthodox Church, and lesser bureaucrats, it lacked a middle class; and these exceptions were for the most part themselves either members of or purveyors to a social hierarchy which culminated in the court. Since industry was undeveloped—even as measured by the existing standards of a Western Europe, where it was still embryonic—a city proletariat in the Marxist sense did not exist, though in some large cities impoverished lower classes did. But the dominant population were peasants, poor, largely unfree, and almost entirely illiterate.

The freeing of the serfs, the sustained pursuit of expansionist objectives and the search for an ice-free port, the laying of the trans-Siberian railroad, the struggle for a parliament, and the organization of radicalism and of revolutionary parties all lay in the future. So, too, did the building of those few large industrial enterprises which existed prior to the Revolution and the official attempts to adapt Western skills and organization which preceded World War I.

The contrasts between past and present in Russia are even more startling than in the United States. An imaginative perception of their import for agrarian peoples is vital to the understanding of the appeal of the Russian way and, thus, to a sound assessment of Russia's strength. Despite setbacks and German destruction in World War II, Russia has established large-scale modern industries, has taught masses of previously untrained peasants to be industrial workers, and has developed a force of engineers and technicians capable of creating and running such industries. It has built new industrial towns in regions once sparsely inhabited and almost undeveloped. It has unlocked and utilized its own varied mineral resources. It has, at horrible human cost, developed modern large-scale mechanized agriculture. It has developed internal communications to tie its empire and economy together, as it has developed city transport systems and the public services of modern cities. It has developed bureaucracies for government, not less than for industry, of an efficiency undreamed of under the czars. It has reduced illiteracy with extraordinary thoroughness and rapidity. It has made books, movies, theatres, opera, ballet, and other cultural goods effectively available to very large numbers of people sprung from classes which once enjoyed neither leisure nor culture. It has, within its own hierarchies, provided careers open to talents. It has created genuine opportunity for persons who, under the old regime, had no hopes of rising, of developing valued skills, and of attaining positions of leadership or prestige. It has brought its own backward and subject peoples within the ambit of modern civilization and, however much it has maltreated them in the name of service to Communist dogma, it has shown interest and pride in their native cultures. In general, it has demonstrated an ability to adapt and use Western scientific knowledge and Western organizational skills in the development of a country previously backward and dominantly agrarian and to apply them alike to the needs of peace and the exigencies of war. It has shown that power and prestige can be gained by its methods and inferior status overcome.

The American task

To deny the reality of these achievements would be both foolish and futile. It would be foolish because it would prevent us from understanding the bases of pride and morale among the peoples of the Soviet Union and of Soviet appeal to other peoples who now stand where Russians stood only yesterday. It would be futile because it would convict us of incomprehension in the eyes of both the Russian and the satellite peoples. It would indeed confirm their leaders' insistence that we are deliberately hostile from malevolence and inhumanity and from envious resentment of their great accomplishment which we are determined to destroy because, in rate and reach, it exceeds our own. For the Soviet people, like any other, looks backward to where it was in past generations. In that perspective its achievements—especially to men who have no experience whereby to assess what to the Westerner are grim costs—seem to warrant a pride in the collectively self-made nation analogous to that earlier American boastfulness which once so distressed more settled and sophisticated Europeans. Neighboring peoples of like moral inexperience of Western freedom, but with similar experience of mass miseries in populous agrarian societies, quite intelligibly contemplate the Russian achievement with envy; desire to achieve equally rapid development; tend, because of a not dissimilar past, to be predisposed to follow the Russian course and pattern; and are initially impressed by seemingly generous promises of leadership and sharing made by the Soviet rulers. It is therefore vital for us to demonstrate, in terms that those so deluded can understand on the basis of their own experience, first that the Russian achievement is less impressive and the Russian promise more delusive than they superficially appear; and secondly that we can offer a real and relevant alternative without the Soviet drawbacks.

By Western criteria, Russian industry may indeed be inefficient, the people's living standards still miserably low, the diffusion of culture inadequate. To demonstrate the superiority of the West in all these respects is important in order to show that the Russian doctrine of inevitable capitalist decay is nonsense. That demonstration is also relatively easy. Next it is necessary to show that the rate of Russian development has been less startling than it initially appears to be, since Russia could freely borrow the arts and skills of the West, developed at great cost over long time. Moreover, it did not suffer the liabilities of already going concerns and exploited resources. It is likewise necessary to demonstrate that the West, and the United States in particular, has progressed enormously over the same period, in culture not less than in production and distribution. That task is somewhat more difficult, while the gains from its accomplishment are alone insufficient for Western purposes. It is further necessary to demonstrate that the human costs of Russian gains have been inordinately great. To show their reality is simple. To convince peoples who hold individual life less dear than does Western man that such costs were both unnecessary and corrupting is a very different matter. Yet, in order to make clear the lasting evil of Soviet methods, it is imperative to prove that its totalitarian and inhumane means will lastingly pervert its professed ends and prevent their attainment. Moreover, it is necessary to provide such proof in a situation where the growth of cultural goods makes the limitation of their range by imposed censorship seem of minor moment.

Finally, in order to bring conviction that such means were and are unnecessary, it is essential to show that the methods and institutions characteristic of the West can be adapted and used by agrarian, and especially Eastern, peoples. It is vital to show that their use may be expected to bring at least as rapid and good results. It is vital to show that the West understands the needs of such peoples and is prepared to aid them towards its own blessings. Above all, it is vital to persuade those peoples or their leaders that the West does not intend to exact political domination or economic exploitation as the price of its aid.

Historically, the superior achievement and promise of the West is obvious, once they are stated and made known, as the meaning of developments over the last hundred and more years is clear. The Industrial Revolution began in England, somewhere around 1760. But industrialism reached maturity in the United States above all during the present century. Industrial technology now makes available the material basis for fuller realization in the West of the joint ethical and political insights embodied in the Graeco-Roman and Judaeo-Christian traditions. It is likewise the hopeful means to the progressive betterment of the rest of the world. Already the Oriental peoples, bred in very different traditions, desire its blessings and dimly glimpse the higher values to which it is a handmaiden. It is necessary to clarify those values to them and to show them how to achieve those blessings.

At its best, the American way of life reveals the use of technology in the service of such values. Its economic system makes available a rich variety of goods and services. Standards of living, symbolized in average

income, are no longer niggardly. Despite the continuance of great inequalities, that average tends increasingly to rise. In America the class
divisions of an aristocratic agrarian society were never fully established,
while the miseries of early industrialism have been progressively diminished. America has slowly but surely reduced the curse of Adam, and
ordinary men have come to enjoy an amplitude of leisure never before
known in the world. Those developments have together given men
liberty and human dignity. For their consequence is effective opportunity for fulfillment of the needs, and expression of the endowments,
of diverse personalities.

Peoples still agrarian, whether in Eastern Europe or Asia, not un-
naturally resent, envy, and strive to attain the American standard of
living. In particular, the vast masses of Asia live a life of malnutrition
which, in its brevity, is reminiscent of Hobbes' state of nature and a
warrant for Malthusian gloom. They want American products and,
where possible, seek eagerly to get them. Their leaders desire to introduce
industrial technology as a means to provide such goods yet equally
desire to avoid utter social disruption during the period of transformation. Their task is exceedingly difficult. For the Anglo-American
heritage of free institutions was no painless achievement, and the ways
of a free and self-disciplined society are hard for simple and politically
untrained peoples to emulate successfully.

Western Europe, whose nations are either industrialized or within the
ambit of the industrial economy and ethos, presents a different problem. For, as measured by the United States, those nations have declined in at least their relative enjoyment of the standards of industrial
society. That decline is due variously to lack of resources, to exhaustion
of resources, to antiquated equipment and inadequate capital, and to
devastation and deaths in war. As a result, the Western European peoples are to some degree politically or economically dependent on the
United States. Such dependence is hurtful to pride, especially given
memories of past glories and leadership. Consequently, it begets resentment. Yet these peoples have not hitherto been reduced to despair.
Moreover, by training and heritage they are more capable than the
Eastern European peoples of the political life of free men. At a minimum,

they are devoted to its ideals through long aspiration to its realities. Their question is whether it is possible through the method of freedom to restore or develop economies which will enduringly provide the security and living standards indispensable to stable democracy. Uncertain of the answer, they teeter between the alternatives of a grim and imposed discipline more suited to, or bearable by, non-Westernized peoples and a democratic freedom which entails a long and harsh struggle of uncertain outcome.

The Communist undertaking

Such conditions in Asia and Europe provide a context for assessment of the U.S.S.R. and for evaluation of its appeal. Quite early in its history, Russia became loosely related to the West by the common possession of Christianity; though the differences in organization and creed of the Eastern and Western churches also constituted barriers, as they reflected basically disparate social-political orders. Since the days of Peter the Great, Russia has intermittently faced westward in a search for the techniques and ideologies by which to modernize and gain effective power. But the Revolution of 1917 ushered in the first sustained attempt to borrow and adapt to Russia's political and economic purposes the knowledge and the production techniques of the contemporary West. In the course of its transforming settlement, the Revolution became increasingly sinister as it lost ethical ardor and imposed a lasting dictatorship in a one-party state. But, as noted above, it developed organizational effectiveness. It successfully imposed on a backward people the severe discipline that transformed them into industrial workers and farm hands. The immediate objective was to bring about the rapid development and utilization of resources by adapting and using the production techniques and the massing of capital goods characteristic of advanced Western technology. The dominant purpose was to attain equality with the West in capacity to produce, in standards of living, and in political power. The hope and promise to the people was that the Soviet system would in due course far outstrip the West in these respects.

The Revolution was, in name, Communist. In fact, it was a twofold revolution—against an *ancien régime,* and for industrialism. Neither of its interdependent parts was related to the overthrow of capitalism as a general system, since, in the Marxian sense of the term, such a system had never burgeoned in Russia. Revolution, therefore, did not come first in Russia, as Lenin had argued it might come first in an agrarian country, because Russia was "the weakest link in the capitalist chain." As a revolution to destroy an *ancien régime,* it manifestly was not first at all. In a certain sense, indeed, it was belated. For that regime had uneasily combined Western absolutism and Oriental despotism. It had failed to use fully the elements of creative ordering characteristic at certain stages of the former, by reason of the inefficient unprogressiveness normally associated with the latter. There was, therefore, even more warrant for revolution in Russia in 1917 than there had been in France in 1789.

No less manifestly, Russia's was not the first industrial revolution. Yet industrialization under the Communists did involve a novel undertaking. For, through a system of soviets and through enforced plans, the party leadership sought to industrialize a predominantly agricultural country and to transform backward farming methods so that agriculture would support the necessary force of industrial workers. The area involved was huge, the population vast and illiterate. Despite the abolition of feudalism half a century before, remnants of feudal economy and more than remnants of feudal psychology had survived. An economy based on status and customary productive techniques was to be forcibly made into a modern industrial and agricultural order marked by the acceptance of innovation and the deliberate use of invention. The nation's productive population had to move from the accustomed routines and rhythms of the seasons to the mechanical tempo and the disciplined attention of the factory. In essence, Lenin initiated and Stalin executed a design rapidly to change a society used to the way of life of pre-industrial centuries into the equivalent in technology, industrial organization, and know-how of the most advanced capitalist nations in the age of the corporation, the cartel, and the assembly line. To leap so far involved daring and vision, as well as extreme ruthlessness. Success in the undertaking was bound to appeal to the imagination, to command the attention, and to relate to the interests, of other agrarian peoples.

Moreover, while the revolution was not communistic in its consequences, Marx and Marxism were neither irrelevant to its conduct nor unimportant for the bolstering of its appeal elsewhere. Marx himself had accepted the fact that industrial technology was here to stay. He had rejected the yearnings of many of his contemporary ethical and romantic critics of industrialism for a return to a simpler world. Indeed, he and his heirs contemptuously dubbed such seekers pre-scientific socialists, not altogether without justification. For Marx perceived that the industrial order could prove the liberating means to the most effective pursuit of man's lasting and fundamental ethical insights. He insisted, likewise, that its harnessing of physical power and its use of applied science constituted bases for political power and superior military force. He realized that peoples who possessed industrial technology, not less than classes who controlled its use, enjoyed a privileged position in the world.

Lenin learned this lesson. He understood that power for Russia and well-being for the Russian people alike depended on industrialization; and he was ready to sacrifice his own and the succeeding generation to its attainment. Trotsky, though he agreed on the need, came to feel that the means would either pervert the ethical end or prevent its attainment. He fell from power, fled, and, some years later, was assassinated in Mexico City. Stalin, who by skillful intrigue had made himself Lenin's successor, was more power-hungry than Lenin, but less imaginative and enlightened in objective. He continued to use the ideal of Marxist Communism as a convenient myth at home and as effective propaganda abroad. Nevertheless, in policy he increasingly stressed Russian acquisition and use of power as a nation. Nor (despite expedient concessions) has Malenkov changed the basic Stalinist policies.

Repeatedly, however, the Soviet regime has emphasized the teaching (implicit in Marx and made explicit by Lenin) that nonindustrialized countries are subject to exploitation. Their peoples necessarily remain unsatisfied and underprivileged until they have rejected all dependence on capitalist powers and have advanced along the road to industrialism under Communist auspices. These doctrines early proved a powerful basis of appeal for support of the regime in Russia itself and have lastingly helped sustain Russian morale. Subsequently, they have appealed to large parts of Asia where they have been skillfully reconciled with nationalist aspirations, which they have even reinforced.

The resultant doctrine is not unlike Mussolini's emendation of Marx, whereby class struggle became the struggle between have and have-not nations. It lacks, however, the statist underpinnings of that tour de force. It emphasizes the universalist professions of Marxism, but posits Russia as natural leader in the inevitable struggle. It is addressed to peoples conspicuously beyond the European industrial ambit. It carries the promise that, through dictatorship and discipline, these peoples can enjoy an ultimate well-being as individuals and can gain a more immediate collective and public status of parity with the white race and with Western industrial nations. Communism brought Russia the power and benefits of Western industrialism without reliance on Western capital; without the need to go through the long, slow process of Western industrial evolution; without Western intervention and dominance; and, indeed, without dependence on Western ambitions or reliance on the motivations of Western capitalism. Asiatic and East European agrarian peoples may have like benefits, as some are stated to be getting them, by accepting Communist teaching and the aid and protection of its legitimate exponent, the Soviet Union. In this context the often preposterous claims of Russia to priority in scientific discovery and superiority in scientific theory and practice take on new meaning: they are persuasive propaganda to give these peoples, as well as the Russians themselves, assurance of the reality of such emancipation and of the certainty of progress.

Such, then, has been the value in actual use of Marx's teaching as to the superiority of the industrial order. His doctrine of social justice, to be fully realized in the classless society, has been equally valuable as myth and as builder of morale. In Russia itself, men had to be weaned away from the unthinking routines of agrarian life. They had to be changed and trained to operate machinery and to work in teams with their fellows. New patterns of behavior had to be rapidly substituted for old. It was necessary to achieve a release of men's creative energies in positive action. It was necessary to get a general and willing acceptance of the discipline needful to industrialization and the sustained functioning of an industrial order. Punishments and compulsion based on force alone were not enough. It was vital to evoke and nurture an enthusiasm grounded in purpose and directed to a goal. The promise and bright vision of a classless society constituted such a goal and performed the function of a Sorelian myth, whereby the vision of the desirable end, in truth impossible, nevertheless girded and goaded men to creative and purposive action. It inspired humble men by assurances of destiny and of righteousness.

As time went on, and the leaders progressively lost revolutionary ardor and gained a taste for power and its privileges, the day for attaining the goal had to be put into an ever more distant future. Supposed threats from capitalist powers then proved an explanation and an inspiration to a loyalty which neatly combined mass ambitions and national attachment; and this combination appeared fully warranted by the German invasion of World War II. Marx's teachings of the necessity of class struggle and of the inescapable inherent contradictions within capitalism seemed under the circumstances to justify delays in attainment of the ideal. They strengthened and clarified an immediate purpose. They gave an assured conviction of victory in the world. They clearly indicated that Russia, rather than the United States or Western Europe, would first secure the gains of industrialization for the bulk of the population. Moreover, with the help of an Iron Curtain supposedly necessary for protection of the Soviet people against class enemies, these doctrines hid the fact that much of the Western world, and especially the United States and Great Britain, had in recent times moved rapidly towards the enjoyment of the values of a genuinely classless society. The achievements of constitutional democracy, which effectively reconciled individual freedom and enterprise with the public promotion and protection of social welfare, were cavalierly ignored and cleverly hidden. Marxist doctrine served the régime by helping to conceal the availability elsewhere of a leisure and a high level consumption which were either beyond Russia's existing capacity to provide or were deliberately withheld and refused by its leadership. It helped to persuade the people that they themselves were better off and to reconcile them to shortages held to be the consequence of a bitter struggle against vicious, corrupt, and doomed opponents.

In the postwar years, these teachings of an inescapable but inevitably triumphant struggle and of an ultimately sure fulfillment have continued to be proffered elsewhere. Where the Soviet has imposed its power or achieved hegemony, they have proved useful as the rationale for enforced collectivization and as a spur to industrialization. In Western Europe, such teachings and hopes are appealing wherever the experience of workers has been that of bitter poverty insufficiently alleviated by social reform. They may prove convincing if hopes for progress and reconstruction under other auspices appear unlikely to succeed.

The orientation of American policy

The circumstances, conditions, and ideas outlined above constitute a momentous problem for American foreign policy. The nature and strength of Soviet appeal—and the realistic Russian objectives to which such appeal is geared—determine the direction and essential content of policies adequate to our own purposes. Moreover, American policy has to be conducted with an awareness that Western Europe is no longer central to the order of industrial civilization, actual and potential; but that, as the origin and sharer of our ways, it is our most probable and valuable ally and our first line of defense against aggression. Yet our policy cannot regard Europe as the center of the universe. It generated, indeed, the rationalist science, the technology, and the ideologies at the root of the present global and bipolar struggle. But their very triumph contained the seeds of Europe's own decay; and it now suffers the fate of costly pioneering while others reap the rewards.

Present-day political economy is inescapably global in scope. The minimal unit of political organization capable of dealing effectively with the issues raised by such an economy is the subcontinental state. The nation-states contained in that smallest of subcontinents, the European peninsula, are simply inadequate to the task, whether their strength be measured by population, resources, or technical efficiency. Nor are they able, as they were in the past, to place sure reliance on supplementary resources derived from overseas empires. At the best, a Europe which had attained effective union might hope to be one subcontinental state among several.

In any event, at the moment the greatly powerful states are Russia and the United States. Despite their radical differences, they have in a certain sense shared a common development whose nature illumines and explains Tocqueville's prophecy that they would divide the world. Both adhered to the state system of Europe in its ascendancy. Both did so as a matter of defense against, and influence in, that system. Both borrowed greatly from it; though the borrowings and, even more, the uses made of them differed radically. Yet each participated and emulated only so that it might pursue a different adventure and look beyond the horizons of Europe. Indeed, America is more clearly the heir and the future of European civilization (and less the enemy and the rebel against it) than is Russia. America, moreover, is at present the realization of the promise of industrial civilization, whereas the U.S.S.R. is its belated borrower and violently rapid emulator. The current issues of world politics are: who shall be its future custodian; who shall direct and benefit from the spreading of its blessings elsewhere; and what institutions and aspirations shall accompany its introduction? Decisions on these questions are fateful for our own time and for the generations immediately to come. The choice is between the peaceful coexistence of peoples or wars resultant on the imperialism of dogmatic ideology; between respect for human dignity or submission to inhumane oppression in futile pursuit of a perverse utopia. On grounds of reason, bipolar conflict seems unnecessary. Yet, on the basis of actual history, it was well-nigh inevitable. The central misfortune of that history was the convenient presence of Marxism as an *idée maîtresse* for modernizing Russians to borrow and apply.

In 1917, Russia had lost a costly and highly disruptive war to Germany's well organized industrial power. The Bolsheviks learned the lesson and were determined to industrialize their country as rapidly as possible. Their perception of what was needed for power and status in the modern world was clear and correct. In undertaking the task, they decided that, regardless of immediate costs and difficulties, they would not be at the mercy of foreign capital. Whatever the price, they would retain full control of the conditions of Russia's own development. Again, the decision was intelligible. For they had confronted a postwar invasion directed against their Revolution, an invasion in which United States forces had participated. That invasion confirmed the view, at that time not peculiar to Marxists, that foreign investment in undeveloped countries inevitably led to exploitation and denial of independence, either through political imperialism or through a more subtle, but equally sure, dollar diplomacy. Thirdly, it would have been wasteful to strive to assimilate modern industrial technology and organization by means of individual enterprise at home. Indeed, it would have been almost impossible: the country had never possessed many large plants; it had never had a large group of trained technicians; and, in the anger of revolution reinforced by the Marxist dogma that it was necessary to liquidate the bourgeoisie, its revolutionaries had killed off a large proportion of its professional men, its managers and administrators, and its technologists. Under the circumstances, the appropriate techniques for developing a heavy industry and mechanized agriculture after the American model seemed clear. Public ownership of productive instruments and government directed and controlled planning took the place of that private and corporate investment, development and direction possible in America owing to long evolution, accumulation, and training. As a corollary, reliance had to be placed on compulsive political-legal sanctions and on public propaganda rather than on private self-interest and the motivations of the market.

Given some visible success, such methods were bound to have considerable appeal to other peoples in similar circumstances. Wherever the blessings and power of industrialism were desired, available capital limited, and know-how and a trained industrial force virtually absent, forward-looking and modernizing leaders were bound to regard the Russian undertaking and experience with considerable interest. With encouragement and opportunity, many of them would go to Russia to learn about the system. They would study its operation. They would investigate its possibilities for their own countries. Given sympathy and discreet prompting, they would in many cases be convinced. Given aid or the promise of aid, they would themselves become missionaries of the Russian way among their own people. Granted sufficient Russian skill in modifying and adapting Soviet ideas and practices so that they would appeal to other peoples and fit local needs, such peoples might well be converted and become eager to undertake experiments on the Russian model.

The adoption of collectivistic means of creating and running industry in Russia could not properly be a just cause for conflict, for intervention, or for hostility on our part. Nor could we object to the borrowing and emulation of these means by other peoples, nor to Russian assistance to such peoples, provided the assistance were voluntarily sought or accepted. Americans might and do feel that the system is inferior to their own; that it holds less long-term promise as a system of production; and that it gives men far less rewards as consumers and persons. Obviously it lacks the values of democratic freedom which they properly cherish. But, were these their only legitimate objections, it would be incumbent upon them to realize that less fortunate peoples might legitimately use what seemed appropriate means to achieve modernization and well-being rapidly. Americans might pity such peoples for their lack of literacy, of trained skills, of ability to be participants in politics, and of leisure for cultural pursuits. They might also endeavor to persuade them that there were better ways available to achieve their purposes. But we would perceive that disciplined Communism involved an unstated acknowledgement of inferiority and backwardness in comparison with the American political economy. We would then view it as a technique of imposed order and systematic planning to catch up with the latter, both in amplitude of capital goods and in volume of trained industrial manpower.

The peaceful coexistence of two such ways of life would not be inherently impossible, especially since Communism would in truth pay the Western way the compliment of silent recognition of free enterprise's success under democratic government. Under such conditions, it is true, the role of American enterprise would be very limited, or nonexistent, in any area where the Communist technique of modernization came to be chosen. But even though we might hold a universal Open Door policy good for all peoples, and not merely in the interest of our own enterprisers, it would hardly be consonant with our ethics to endeavor to impose it forcefully on others. Nevertheless, the existence of the barriers of a planned economy isolated from the West would limit hopes for the immediate spread of American and Western political ideas and practices and of the ethic of personal development on which they rest. Yet, in the long run, the development of industry and the raising of living standards elsewhere might create the conditions for the ultimate triumph of Western insights and the Western ethos.

Communism's promise that it can rapidly create a modern economic order in backward countries is the very basis of hospitality to it, and towards the U.S.S.R. as its representative. It is welcomed as a means of providing both better living standards and collective status and dignity. Without that welcoming predisposition, the U.S.S.R. would have found its recent expansion extremely difficult. Had it desired to expand, it would have been driven to a purely military imperialism. It would then have achieved the support of quislings alone. It would have possessed even less initial appeal than did Japan with its Co-Prosperity Sphere, and as little lasting success. But the Soviet regime does promise betterment to nonindustrialized peoples. Its appeal on that ground constitutes a fundamental difficulty for American foreign policy. It is, indeed, a basic condition of our conduct in international relations. For, whatever the short-term imperatives, the United States cannot hope to achieve sustained success and enjoy lasting influence by a policy confined to repelling forceful aggression and maintaining an international order of law. Those undertakings are vital and primary. However imperfect the existing legal system, it must be securely maintained as a precondition of its own improvement. But its genuine acceptance by others necessitates our understanding their basic needs and primary aspirations. Such understanding is a precondition of sustained and expanded American moral authority in the world. It is our obligation to recognize the appeal of Communism and to provide alternative means to meet the needs to which it appeals. To be effective, these means must be relevant to the actual conditions of the peoples to be won.

Russian ambition: America's opportunity

That Russia does not simply proffer a theory and practice for the industrial organization and development of hitherto nonindustrialized peoples, but combines with these a policy of forceful aggression and a dogma of irreconcilable hostility to any system not of its making or direction—this is a profound misfortune from the viewpoint of immediate peace, security, and harmony in the world. But that misfortune may provide an otherwise unavailable opportunity for the immediate global promotion of American democratic ideas and social welfare practices. For the Russian undertaking is wedded to Marxist doctrine rendered dogma. Hence it is lastingly and fundamentally destructive of essential human values, as it is now inimical to their present proximate achievement by the United States. Furthermore, in current practice, Marxist dogma constitutes protective coloration for Russian nationalism and is a stalking horse for imperialist expansion.

As previously shown, Marxism neatly fitted the needs of nonindustrial nations in search of modern industry. It was rendered even more useful to that end by Lenin's devising of a theory of strategy and organizational discipline. First calculated to meet the needs of revolutionary activity under autocracy, that theory was equally usable in the ordering of military and industrial armies. But, whatever the organizational usefulness of Marxism, it achieved the latter objective at the cost of fundamental perversions of reason and history. Indeed, Marx's own analysis had embodied current scientistic myth and was an immediate reaction to the prevailing stage of industrialization. That stage, it is true, was characterized by a mass misery and exploitation which were morally repulsive because humanly degrading. But Marx plausibly tied enduring Christian moral insight to the symbol, science. He thereupon argued that the ideal of human liberty and dignity could and would be attained by the overthrow of capitalism. An objective historical necessity, that overthrow was the needful precondition to a full use of technology in the service of humanity. Such full use was not only morally good; it was irresistibly determined, were civilization to survive at all. Marx was blinded by the growth of inequality resulting from new mechanical power, as he was obsessed by a complex of ideas which welded together reason, science, determinism, and history. He did not see that class conflict, a heritage from the hierarchical structure of an aristocratic landed order, was transitional in the industrial order and would be self-liquidating. If class struggle was inherent anywhere it was in the agrarian order of limited productivity. For there the niggardliness of nature and the impotence of man made culture and equality incompatible.

Marx and his major heirs insisted that lasting, inevitable, and increasingly acute conflict between classes was inseparable from capitalism. The Russian Communists, and particularly Lenin, ignored or passionately denounced the partial, yet perceptive and promising, insight into the changed and changing structure of capitalist society contained in the challenge from within their camp of Revisionism. That doctrine, developed in the latter part of the nineteenth century by the German socialist Eduard Bernstein, rested on a clear perception and candid assessment of actual changes in the structure of Western capitalist society. These changes cast doubts on the Marxist prophecy of increasing mass misery and heightened class conflict and, as Bernstein insisted, made it questionable whether communist revolution was necessary, desirable, or even possible, yet alone inevitable. Concession and democratic transition might well be in the cards. Nevertheless, the Russian leaders bitterly rejected such an interpretation and reviled its maker. More generally, they denounced the names and works of those socialists who labored peacefully for socialism through or under the institutions and politics of Bismarck's Germany. They denounced the part-contemporary Karl Kautsky even more fervently because he urged collaboration with representative institutions and participation in democratic party processes as an immediately practicable and desirable road to socialist ends. Finally, Lenin took the root idea of internal class struggle and transferred it to a global arena—any seeming diminution of class conflict and any actual concessions by capitalists in particular nations meant only a sharpening of the contradictions of capitalism and a broadening of the base of its exploitations to include native populations, who thereby become an inherent part of the abused proletariat.

This whole body of doctrine was tenable only on a failure to observe the actual course of Western industrial society or on a total inability or unwillingness to grasp its meaning. The failure also involved a grave misjudgment of its future and potentialities. On that error the U.S.S.R. has based its recent policy and practice. Given such misunderstanding, it was obligatory for the Soviet regime to oppose Western society. Conflict between the two, open or covert, was inevitable. On the Communist interpretation of capitalism, the triumph of Communism—with the U.S.S.R. as exemplar and leader—was assured. Western capitalism would collapse of its own weight, would be overthrown by internal revolutions, or would be defeated in a war which it had itself provoked.

Today, the consequences of these doctrines are Russian intransigence and a promotion of Russian nationalist ambition under the guise of opposition to capitalism and to Western nationalism, which is held to be the corollary of capitalism. Such intransigence and ambition completely destroy the humanitarian devotion and the ethical aspirations which the original communist theory shared with democratic teaching.

Unfortunately, in our resentment and resistance to Russian ambition and Communist dogma, we fail fully to sympathize with agrarian countries which desire to modernize. We fail to be properly aware that they accept Communism because they lack the Western heritage, fortune, and experience. They do not do so from love of Marx or of Russia. We err, therefore, when we do not recognize their right to use institutional forms and practices which as pioneers we happily escaped and would now find unrewarding and anachronistic. The West, and particularly the United States, fails to see that, at bottom, such peoples aspire to our own achievement. They use another path because it seems to proffer a quicker and more direct way. But the Russian leaders, being blinded by their own dogmatism, similarly fail in insight, or at least in appropriate inference. Though they may perceive the nature of aspirations within the Iron Curtain, they are not thereby moved either to acknowledge Western achievement or to respect Western power. They continue to delude themselves with the conviction of Western doom. Thereby they fortify their own conviction that there is no possibility of living together amicably with the West. Likewise, they necessarily create scepticism on our part as to the real value of conferences between our leaders and their own to seek a *modus vivendi*. By their attitude, they provoke conflict as they prepare to take advantage of the anticipated crises of capitalism.

Our superior case

Nevertheless, whatever the follies of the U.S.S.R., the United States grievously hampers its own effectiveness by perverting its essential insights. The dogma of economic individualism, still so widely prevalent here, is a narrowing of a basic and sound teaching—namely, the worth and dignity of personality. In its extreme purity, that dogma is as irrelevant to present day needs as it is unrevealed in our normal practices. Yet its profession obstructs the development of a genuine alternative to Communism in the East and in Western Europe. It lessens our effectiveness in competing for leadership and influence in those areas. It lends verisimilitude and plausibility to the Russian indictment. In hiding and disguising our real lights, it aids the task of the Russian rulers and Chinese Communist leaders and teachers in assuring their own and neighboring peoples that our ways are irrelevant to their needs. By reason of the selfishness which seems to them implicit in the doctrine, it helps convince them that the West is indeed in moral and social decline. Such conviction combines with new national prides and with collective Oriental aspiration to produce a compensatory sense of superiority. It thereby creates a collective *élan vital* by the unfortunate technique of opposition to the very social order whose achievements are actually envied and to be emulated. Failure on the part of others to perceive that our material base is complemented and completed by a moral and cultural superstructure is the root weakness of our position. And their failure is our fault. We have said the things we ought not to have said, and we have failed to say the things we ought to say.

The root need for the effective conduct of American foreign policy is a coherent theory of political ethics and its proper application to political dynamics. Such theory and practice must correspond to our insights and to our achievements. They must reflect, as they must live in, our practices at home. They must constitute the basis of our propaganda, even as they must direct and inspire our actions and aid, abroad.

The setting of American policy is global. Europe has ceased to be the center of world politics, and the European nation-state rapidly ceases, in form and scale, to be the typical or relevant unit of political organization. The subcontinental state is the new, and relevant, institution. For it is the minimum area for the effective operations of industrial societies.

Tocqueville's essential analysis and contrast still holds good today. The leaders in the modern world are the United States and the Union of Socialist Soviet Republics. Both once adhered to the European states system and its conceptual framework, as both once functioned in its ambit and submitted to its limitations. Yet both adhered in order to escape, as both looked outward and elsewhere to broader horizons and a different world.

The one is today the leader in the industrialized order. The other offers leadership in rapid industrialization to countries hitherto unindustrialized, and it points to itself as illustration of what they may hope to accomplish by following its pattern. The one claims that continuity in the evolution of its political and economic institutions is compatible with the full development and use of industrial technology and with the progressive enjoyment of its blessings. The other insists that only through revolution may the full resources of the earth and the full powers of men's minds be successfully combined to free man from the curse of Adam and to permit him fulfillment as a rational and moral being.

Both are agreed on the ultimate goods. They disagree radically on the means to their attainment and on the impediments in the way. They disagree as to the desirability of the utter sacrifice of present men for future generations. They disagree as to whether such sacrifice can avail, can lead to the intended end. The American argues for personal freedom en route; the Russian sees it only at the end. The American sees force as a bitter necessity; the Russian views it as a magnificent creative instrument. The struggle of world politics is to decide which outlook shall prevail.

II

Hindrances to policy: Isolationism

Ideals and impediments

By reason of the power at its command the United States is today the chief proponent of that way of life which is rooted in the values of the Western tradition. Further, it is by heritage and history the most advanced embodiment of those values. It offers them to the world as the real promise of the goods which aspiring men everywhere seek and hope to share. Its task as leader is to generate power through the appeal of those values and to use that power to spread them more widely. It can succeed in such an undertaking only if it first demonstrates that they are vital and creative in its own public and social life. Thereafter it must give others the conviction that it is willing and able, by reason of enlightened interest grounded in its own moral commitment, to support and aid them in their struggle to attain the good life as human freedom from want, and for self-realization.

We, the people of the United States, must therefore reveal—first in our practice at home, and then in our foreign policy—a clear and unswerving positive commitment to democratic constitutionalism, social pluralism, and respect for human personality. For these collectively constitute our heritage and embody our goal. Despite lip-service and good intentions, of late we have failed to hold to our values with clarity and steadfastness. We have not sought and ensued their preservation and furtherance with insight and institutional adaptiveness. We have not revealed to a waiting and critical world an unswerving commitment to our enunciated principles or consequential policies for their implementation. Too often our behavior has evoked suspicions of self-delusion.

The American people have been influenced by the insidious and unrecognized impact of Marxist indictments of capitalism, which they have partially accepted and incorporated into their thinking. They have likewise been too greatly captivated by gloomy critics of moral decadence and prophets of the inevitable decay of Western civilization. Despite the growth of American power, American people have lost much of the convinced self-confidence and belief in a richer material and moral destiny which characterized their progenitors. Loud proclamations of force and of rightness, and indignant denunciations of the evils of Soviet Communism today, as of Fascism yesterday, have a shrill undertone of uncertainty. Domestic policies for dealing with internal threats to our security indicate doubts as to the wisdom of ignoring conspirators on the ground that they are powerless against the strength of our institutions and the integrity of our morale. Yet we are hesitant to use necessary means to protect ourselves against confessed opponents who reject, yet exploit, the method of freedom. For we are unsure of our own values. Consequently, we exaggerate dangers, feel illiberal and guilty in erecting defenses, yet dare not rely on earlier safeguards alone.

The overcoming of doubts and insecurity is not aided by the prevalence of the dogmas of isolationism, individualism, and power politics as national interest. These dogmas are incompatible with our professions, inimical to our institutions, and impediments to successful appeal to others. Among them, power politics is the broadest and most dangerous. Derived from modern Europe, it is a root enemy of those values peculiarly embodied in American institutions. The second, individualism, is a modern—and in the main home-grown—perversion of a sound insight which, while derived largely from the Reformation, came to secular fruition on these shores. The first, isolationism, is likewise a perversion, in this case of a purely American doctrine and practice. It was once legitimate as protection of a new venture; and for long it remained unobjectionable in a world less interdependent than today, wherein we also lacked our present position of power and leadership.

Isolationism is at present the most conspicuous, though not the most serious, impediment to an effective American foreign policy. It reveals most clearly a lack of moral self-confidence and moral purpose on our part. It is the most resented by others and is the primary cause of their legitimate questioning of our will to leadership, and of our capacity to lead. Its roots can be stated, and its fruits displayed and criticized, in brief compass.

Insulation as national interest

As a theory and program for the conduct of foreign policy, isolationism is as simple as it is irrelevant to present American power and contemporary world needs. It is motivated at once by a frightened sense of insecurity, a selfish desire to preserve and enjoy our superior standards of living without concern for others, and a vainglorious conviction that we have the force to protect ourselves fully as we enjoy our way of life alone. The motivations may be logically incompatible with one another. They are most certainly incompatible with the desire to make the rest of the world behave as we would like it to behave. The isolationist seeks to force others to conform to a pattern which at once flatters us by emulation and makes the isolationist course easy by insuring undisturbed order while quietly accepting lasting inequality with us. Those motivations are also incompatible with the simultaneous desire to enjoy freedom of trade with the rest of the world and assured supplies of such things as we lack, including scarce materials necessary for defense and for the smooth functioning of our complex industrial machine. Indeed, isolationism has in it the qualities of a dream world, arrested, stable, static, and, for us, a perfect fulfillment of heart's desire. That dream is also in a sense imperialistic—a belated newcomer to the ranks of world powers, we seek, through this delusive aspiration which professes to be hard-boiled realistic doctrine, to hold the world in fee without revolt, without challenge, and without cost to ourselves. Isolationism looks for the rewards of empire without costs, and without the responsibilities of governing others. It professes that a power which behaves like the proverbial ostrich deserves a comfortable world it never worked to make simply because it possesses the virtues of minding its own business and cultivating its own garden. It proclaims such policy realistic because it involves no commitment and because the force to make withdrawal a practicable undertaking is supposedly available and calculable, whereas any positive commitment is not precisely definable and permanently delimitable. Yet on occasion the isolationist seems to use his dogma not as the sole proper design for American living but as a Damocles' sword which may be allowed to fall on others with disastrous consequences if they do not play the game by rules we impose.

An exposition of the nature and direction of isolationist thinking, combined with a brief statement of current world conditions and of our own actual commitments, would readily dispose of isolationism as a serious theory of foreign policy were the isolationist not able to add to his claim that he alone is realistic, asserting further that his position is uniquely patriotic. He claims not only that he is motivated by an exclusive concern for American interest; he also insists that his teaching is the sole faithful embodiment of our whole tradition and, in particular, of the teachings and strivings of the Founding Fathers. Despite the debunking of that line of appeal, a people who have lived under a written constitution which is often construed by reference to the intent of its makers are still apt to find such argument persuasive. Indeed, our lack of conservatism grounded in institutions and our revolutionary origins make us all the more conservative in such veneration. As the French appeal to their Revolution and to the principles of 1789, so we turn to George Washington and to the other worthies who made our Revolution and created an operative constitution. And, unlike the French, we lack an earlier national tradition and culture which may be used as a countervailing power in the appeal to history.

To combat the isolationist claim to exclusive legitimate custody of a venerated heritage, it is therefore necessary to demonstrate that, on a careful assessment, these early teachings and their legitimate later uses do not properly lead to the current isolationist program and are even, in intent and accomplishment, alien to it. Since the words and phrases to which the isolationist appeals, and which he repeats, are indeed to be found in the Fathers and in American policy long thereafter, the combatting of current isolationism must rest on appeal to their context and demonstration of the radical differences in the situation to which they were intended to apply and America's contemporary position.

Such demonstration is both legitimate and adequate. For the policies of the statesman, unlike the principles of the philosopher, are intended for application in particular circumstances, or at most under closely similar conditions. Certainly the practical policy-maker does not seek to emulate Deity or from his rostrum or cabinet to give forth edicts as universally valid as the Commandments dictated to Moses on Mount Sinai. He may seek, indeed, to instruct his immediate successors; he does not aim, and indeed some of our Fathers noted that they did not aim, to prescribe for conditions they could not, for all their wisdom, foresee.

The earlier insistence that we must not embroil ourselves in European affairs nor allow European powers to intervene in the political life of this continent was a recognition that we were a new country. Our resources were undeveloped. Our population in relation to territory was scanty. The force at our command was barely adequate to security within our borders. Our westward vision, gained so early in our life as a nation, was majestic. It required undistracted and undisturbed devotion of all our energies to render the aspiration reality. Hence, our desire to isolate ourselves from Europe was in truth a conscious rejection of a futile and misguided direction and use of our energies, on the one hand, and a deliberate statement of the conditions needful to their most effective employment, on the other.

Our policy in the whole period down to the end of the geographical frontier, with some few exceptional adventures themselves largely designed to protect our venture and insure against hampering limitations in its execution, may properly be called continental insulationism. We were not isolationist, in the sense of unconcern for Europe or a desire to enjoy higher standards of living in callow selfishness. We had indeed the vision of a better, freer, happier world to be created from a European heritage through America's liberating opportunity. With dignified humility, we saw that we could not aid or improve Europe directly; we would only embroil ourselves, misuse our resources, and invite its intervention here were we to meddle in its politics. At the same time, we sought to gain and keep exclusive control of our own subcontinental territory that we might shape it to our design and heart's desire. We desired to avoid the divisions, the conflicts of powers, and the social and political institutions characteristic of European life. Moreover, we sought, both as an extension of that insurance and from an interest in a like freedom for our neighbors, likewise to prevent further incursions or extensions of territorial possessions by European powers in this hemisphere. Our insulationism was essentially a doctrine of proportionality of responsibility to power under conditions of relative weakness, distance, and slow communications. For these prohibited direct political leadership in the world but permitted the influence of an example of superior happiness were we circumspectly, yet forthrightly, to use our unique opportunity. We hoped, by building a better world here at home, not only to enjoy the rewards of our energies and fortune but to shape the destinies of all Western culture. Proud of our superior promise and, later, performance, we were not too proud to share. Our land was open to those who would come, and our ways were theirs to borrow if they would. Unable to aid those of greater power and accumulated wealth, we stood ready to encourage and applaud and to give refuge in time of stress. But, however exalted our growing national pride, we saw ourselves as a repository of universal values; and we were fully conscious of a duty, and even a mission, to mankind. But we were not yet a great power, and we did not live in a tight-knit, interconnected, and interdependent world.

Yet, for the sake of sustaining independence, and on behalf of maintaining a deliberate difference in outlook and interests, this country found itself obligated to identify with the European state system. It was necessary to seek inclusion in it and to claim parity as a participating member. Subsequently, it was important, in order to conduct policy effectively, so to organize internal affairs as to strengthen the sense of being a people. It was vital to beget an American loyalty. It was imperative to secure a geographical area which could be transformed by possession and development into an American heartland. The overriding objective and interest and the basic concept of policy were insulation.

Our own bloodless revolution, by which the Articles of Confederation were jettisoned and the Constitution substituted after hard and sometimes bitter debate, was an act of policy in the national interest. It properly treated our internal organization and development—and our security and status in the world—as interdependent. That Constitution was necessary to security as a means to insure lasting national freedom. It provided a basis for an internal and external credit that would promote prosperity and power. In the structure it established, not less than in the guarantees of rights which were the condition of its acceptance, it also affirmed and furthered the peculiar nature of the American enterprise. That enterprise was a social-political order which sought the values, without the drawbacks, of the European state. From the beginning ours was a public-welfare society, and not merely a political power order.

The Hamiltonian system was a logically necessary step in insulationist policy. For England was developing an industrial order which could profitably export manufactured goods in exchange for raw materials. Were the United States to remain dominantly agricultural, relying on England for such goods, its political independence would have profited little. It would still be in essence a dependent colony. Hamilton sought to avoid that situation. *His intent was not, it is important to note, isolationist.* Nor was his policy designed to produce what a later age was to designate as "autarky." The "infant-industries" argument rested upon an acceptance of the general theory of international free trade. It simply stated that special circumstances warranted temporary imposition of protective tariffs. Its logic was free interchange in an industrialized world of equals; protection was a means to attain the equality which would make freedom meaningful. The subsequent problem of divergence between the interests of national power and of personal profit was not envisioned. A hidden hand made the acquisition of national strength and the well-being of individual American enterprisers perfectly consonant. Hamilton's tariff policy was for the moment a statement of special American conditions and opportunities. These once more necessitated following a European (in this case, English) lead by a then peculiarly American method in order to attain an American, and very different, objective. Whatever the subsequent misuses of the "seepage-downward" theory of economic well-being, the underlying doctrine was then quite different from the chasteningly moralistic economics soon to be created by Malthus, Ricardo, and Nassau Senior in England. Men in America could rise upward readily. Protection would broaden their chances and increase their numbers. English political economy, the science justly dubbed "dismal," was, in its post-Smithian formulations, the enemy of social hope. Hamilton's teaching, granted its defense of privilege, and despite the harsh overtones of his own political psychology, was very friendly to the release of the widespread energies that might help to make a nation.

In any event, the Hamiltonian system posited the development of manufactures as a basis for equality with European states and, thus, of sustained independence. To remain merely a supplier of raw materials, Hamilton saw, was to remain colonial, whatever our nominal independence and nationhood. In the short run, the United States would lack secure control of its own internal affairs and development. In the long run, formal independence would itself be jeopardized. Late in life, and with real regret, Jefferson found himself forced to acknowledge the correctness of this thesis. He was driven to abandon the ideal of a purely agrarian society as a possibility for the coming age. To protect his vision, he was forced to advocate a balanced political economy, wherein industry would be sufficiently strong to secure national independence, but not so dominant as to threaten the independence of the person.

Jefferson foresaw the danger that industrialism would destroy the basis of freedom for the individual by turning him into a factory hand and a city dweller. Such a course would lead back towards the hierarchy of European society. It would make the United States an extension of Europe rather than a new and unique societal undertaking. Admittedly, his purpose was sound. But the very contradiction between means and ends which he was forced to acknowledge indicated the limits of his solution. More importantly, with industrialism accepted, the whole subsequent history of the United States has been a search to discover the requisite conditions for personal independence and dignity within that system. Central issues of our politics have been how to gain the national benefits of technological power; how to escape the subordination of the citizen as a subject of the reified nation-state conceived as a power order; and how to prevent the reduction of the mass of men to instruments of the wills of those who control industry and state. Functional distinctions and the inequalities consequent thereon have been continuously accepted. But this country has steadily looked towards, and has always partially achieved, the ideal of a classless society. That ideal, which rested upon constitutionalism in politics and individual and group freedom in society, was the underpinning of insulationism. Membership in the European comity of nations was a technique for preserving and furthering an adventure in separation and departure from the European way of political-economic life.

In this context, Washington's admonition in his Farewell Address where he warned against entangling alliances, the celebrated and much-analyzed Monroe Doctrine, and Jefferson's Louisiana Purchase, all become coherent parts of one whole. Washington's statement was clearly a recognition of the danger that this country, independent and by then generally recognized as part of the comity of nations, might be drawn back into the orbit of European politics. In the process, it might lose the uniqueness of purpose which was the object of its membership to protect and further. The danger that partisanship on our part might lead to conflict with some European power or to a justified European intervention was real enough. But entanglement meant something more than danger from without; it implied involvement from within. It connoted a wrong orientation and a falsified view on the part of the new nation of its own nature, direction, and destiny. Again, the dominant idea was insulation—Washington already indicated awareness of the special character of the American way of life. Later that awareness was to turn into a distrust of Europe, compounded out of American feelings both of inferiority and of superiority. The ultimate corruption of that awareness was an ostrich-like isolationism.

Immediately, the Monroe Doctrine reinforced, broadened, and gave specific content to insulationism. It foreshadowed Pan-Americanism, even as it proclaimed the United States' bid for leadership in the new continents. Above all, it was an endeavor to create an extended boundary for the protection of the American adventure. It sought to secure further insulation from invasions and contagion by the European political state system. The technique was European and smacked of the ideas of balance of power or spheres of interest. But the ethos was not. Whatever the intent of British statesmanship, the United States for over a century was not a new world called in to redress the balance of the old; it was a new adventure to be protected from the uneasy balancings of the old.

The Louisiana Purchase, antedating Monroe's proclamation by two decades, was the more immediate insurance of that protection, as it was the initial key to an internal expansion and development. Essentially, whatever its unintended consequences in subsequent sectional conflict, it provided a major starting point for a societal adventure which fixed forever America's departure from European concepts of statecraft and social organization; even as the Lewis and Clark expedition raised the sights—and prophetically indicated the metes and bounds—of the undertaking. For the rest, the Rush-Bagot treaty, with the consequent demilitarization of our Canadian border, was the moral equivalent of the Monroe Doctrine in the major, and most potentially dangerous, area where prior fact made that doctrine imperfectly applicable. Its consequence was to ensure the needed insulationism. The process, it may be noted, was completed by the pacific settlement, through arbitration, of the Oregon boundary dispute.

Early sectionalism, with the South in the role of nationalist and westward-looking leader, and with maritime-trading New England in part unconcerned and looking to Europe and the high seas, indicated the degree to which the nation was not one in interest. It showed that insulationism was imperfectly developed. Moreover, the South's own agrarian and cotton economy, based on raw materials export and dependence on foreign manufactured imports, made that region itself an inadequate proponent of such a concept of interest.

Overt sectional conflict resulted from the dominance of King Cotton; from the expansionist drive of slavery; from the North's gradual looking inward and westward; and from the West's uneasy awareness that its future was tied to the East rather than to the South. The conflict ultimately proved clarifying, rather than confusing, from the viewpoint of the initial concept of America and its destiny. The strictures by the South on the early industrialism in the North were no doubt just, even as the South's defense of its own system as an organic society of benevolent trusteeship was clever. But, in fact, that slave and estate system which the South wished to extend was clearly an enemy of the American idea of an open and classless society. The South appealed, it is true, to Jeffersonian teaching, which it transformed and applied with real ingenuity. But it sought to establish an hierarchical society equivalent in ethos, though not in intent, to the political-social order of Europe. More importantly still, the South was dependent on English markets to dispose of its great crop. It deeply resented its quasi-colonial dependence on the North, which through protection made it pay dearly for finished products. It was grimly determined and inescapably fated to be a colonial producer of raw materials. Quite intelligibly, it was unwilling to bear the costs of high protectionism. As a consequence, it was opposed to any thoroughgoing practice of an insulationist policy aimed at effective independence for internal development. For long it accepted tariffs with what it deemed self-denying generosity. But it was intransigent in opposition alike to their principle and to the interests which promoted them. The defeat of the South in the Civil War was therefore a further step in this nation's political and economic severance from dependence on Europe, and especially England. The sympathy for the South and the desire of much of the British ruling class to assist the South is here indirect testimony. But the refusal of English workers, despite seeming immediate interest, to follow that line unwittingly facilitated the continuance and completion of earlier American policy concerning this continent.

Men like Calhoun had desired to tie South and West by railroad, and the quarrels leading to the Civil War turned largely on control of the West. But the dominant North-South lines of communication of earlier times had lost their primacy already before the Civil War, though rail routes, which largely ran East-West, had not generally penetrated beyond the Appalachians. The Mississippi, which was later to enjoy a belated revival, had indeed been a major gateway to the Midwest. Yet its course was tangential to straight transcontinental traffic; and despite its vastness, it went but half way. The Civil War decided that traffic should run dominantly East-West, across a full continent. It should interrelate agriculture and industry, with the latter dominant. Initially there was brought into being a new area of rich supplies of raw materials, especially foodstuffs, for the tight-packed industrial nations of Europe. But the long-term development was the American industrial city and the interdependence of internal markets.

Europe became above all a source of manpower for the new internal venture. Under the conditions of free land and undeveloped resources, that import doubly strengthened this country, by numbers and by wealth production. Hence it furthered the attainment of American equality of status with the European nations, sought from the Declaration on. Moreover, it strengthened the peculiarly American adventure, not less by reason of the character and motives of the immigrants— brought by poverty and oppression, and in search of a larger life—than through the activity and opportunity of the environment. The subsequent symbol of the great continental market was testimony to the coming of age of insulationism. So, too, for all the abuses of the Gilded Age, were the primacy of economic undertakings, the subordination of statesmanship, and an essentially pragmatic view of human well-being completely alien to the European concepts of the nation-state. The course of development may be traced from Horace Greeley's celebrated advice and Whitman's "O Pioneers," on the one hand, to Sandburg's "Chicago" and the schools of Midwestern literature on the other. The psychological center, as well as the center of population, moved west. The Midwest, sharing the rich diversity which was an essential of American society, was ever full of politics. But it was long unconcerned with State Department. Symbolically and actually, it constituted the core of a political economy which emphasized democratic welfare and culture developed at home, as against the magnificence of nation-state power.

From insulation to isolationism

Yet the attainment of long-lived objectives of American policy itself involved potentialities for a corrupting transformation from insulation to isolation. Development of home resources became the conspicuous task. Its consequence was the abandonment of statecraft as the proper calling of able men and the enthronement of business activity. Pioneering newcomers first were driven to urgent work to conquer an environment, and then sought to enjoy the immediate fruits of that conquest in contentment. That sequence was the essential process of Americanization for the alien who came here to seek a well-being forever denied him in Europe. The process was highly successful by reason of his general lack of concern for the doings of the rulers of Europe, his resentment of conditions left behind, and his sense of achievement or possible achievement here. Indeed, the denial of freedom to enter and reside in this country, the last step in insulationist policy, was designed (however mean and narrow the motivations of many of its supporters) to give control and protection for an American pattern and level of life. In asserting the superiority of that way, exclusionism involved a denial of its universal availability. It envisaged a protected isolation for its beneficiaries, who were to be concerned only with American welfare. Superficially a continuation and completion of the policies of Hamilton and Clay, its ethos was radically different. The issue was no longer protection to secure equality of status for the new nation and to permit its peculiar development. The objective became a self-interested enjoyment of its special social vision, along with a higher economic level than others possessed. The new concept was the superior American standard of living. Its essence was not promise for all, but privilege for some, to be secured by isolation and exclusion.

Pride in burgeoning American practical skills, today called know-how; a conscious republicanism which found aristocracies and monarchies politically unacceptable; and a re-shaping of the search for cultural independence—these things reinforced the trend. The consciousness of difference in America's objectives was indeed ancient. Its roots were already present in Washington's *Farewell Address*. But the assumptions of the eighteenth and the early part of the nineteenth centuries had been that we inherited and shared European culture, as we inherited and transformingly developed the high calling of the statesman. Emerson, in his celebrated Phi Beta Kappa address, in 1837, on "the American Scholar," was to plead for a cultural declaration of independence. That independence, however, was to be achieved through equality of achievement and the substitution of emulation for imitation. It was not to involve indifference to our cultural heritage nor lack of consumption of the best contemporary cultural products of Europe.

Similarly, on the political side our objectives had long been radically different from Europe's. But it was only in the post-Civil-War period that Europe's politics became generally alien. The growth of European imperialism in Africa and Asia added to the alienation, despite the emulative admiration belatedly exhibited by Theodore Roosevelt. With the balance of political power moving westward, the still young Republic (which Tocqueville had once predicted would a century later sway the destinies "of half the globe") became enamored of the myth of log cabin to White House. Its people consciously glorified humble origins, even as they reduced politics from its earlier primacy. Normal leadership in public life by the educated, the rich, and the well-born of an earlier day ceased to be its practice. Indeed, such leadership was often held undesirable either because it constituted waste of talents which could be better employed in more creative economic activities or from suspicions of the motives and the culture of more successful or privileged persons. Finally, in the latter part of the nineteenth century, American practical inventiveness brought a general independence from European skills, even a sense of American superiority. The conviction was largely warranted by the conspicuous organizational triumph of standardized mass production.

The pattern of movement towards isolationism as apartness, superiority, and suspicion was not indeed a simple, exclusive, and uniform one. Moreover, its development involved seeming logical contradictions which were yet psychologically compatible. Thus cultural nativism was reinforced, rather than combatted, by an awkward sense of America's cultural inferiority. The praise of the superiority of the natural manners of democracy went hand in hand with touchiness in the face of European criticism and with a hectic concern to emulate its "correct" ways. Pride in mass-produced goods was complemented by a snobbish cult, and not merely by a just appreciation, of European custom-made imports. Political exasperation at monarchical states or incomprehension of their ways were not incompatible with love of European titles. Criticism and revelation of these attitudes is neatly interlarded in those works of Mark Twain, for example, concerned with the European scene. By the turn of the century the isolationist psychology was already present. It was compounded of power, achievement, and a sense of superiority, on the one hand, and of an uncertainty, a desire to defer to Europe, and a sometimes pathetic eagerness for approval by Europeans, on the other.

Meanwhile, the very success of rapid internal development and orientation begot the need for regulation of expressions of individualism. It necessitated purification of the special heritage of America. From Populism and Progressivism, the path led to the New Freedom. Retrospectively, this development may appear as a belated American step towards the social-welfare state, already far advanced in much of Europe. But, with all due deference to technological and economic determinists, it was in fact peculiarly American and independent. It used government, but it most conspicuously rejected both statist and socialist concepts. It was not consciously isolationist, but rather a proper inner development of insulationism. Yet it proved perfectly compatible with the "He-kept-us-out-of-the-war" campaign, and indeed constituted its seedbed. That campaign, though loosely related to the obverse side of the Monroe Doctrine, very clearly had emotionally isolationist undertones. Subsequent participation in the European conflict was no doubt due to another, and partially countervailing, lasting strand in American policy, namely a concern for a world of law and peace. Yet some support for participation came from two related drives. First, many Americans had an exasperated sense that Europe, with its alien politics and disturbing policies, must be tidied up and straightened out. It must be urged towards an American pattern by being made safe for democracy in order that this country could live undisturbed on its own. Secondly, some Americans desired to prove to Europe, not less than to ourselves, our superiority as organizers and trouble shooters.

The postwar triumph of the "little band of stubborn men," who yet represented a widely prevalent American viewpoint, constitutes sure evidence on this matter, all questions of personal and partisan politics aside. Moreover, though much of the support of the League of Nations rested on universalist ethics, as some rested on a conscious awareness of the status of American power and consequent inescapable responsibility, a good deal of the internationalism which marked the postwar years was simply a desire to complete the job begun before retiring to cultivate our own garden. Isolationism, in any event, came of age at the very moment when a favorable balance of trade had rendered insulationism itself in no sense longer necessary or effectively serviceable to American welfare.

The inter-war years were no doubt marked by an intermixture of motives, and by resultant policies which lacked coherence. But from the war-debts issue to the involuntary internal concentration and conscious disgust with Europe of the depression years, one major factor in forming our attitudes was the conviction that American achievement was due to superiority, not to good fortune or resources. Similarly, Europe's failures were held to be the consequences of ill will or fecklessness. This general viewpoint undoubtedly reinforced isolationist feeling, even where it begot conviction (increased by Nazism) that the cleaning-up job was still far from complete. Here again the slow progress towards intervention achieved by Roosevelt through calculated propaganda, and the fact that participation came finally through Japan's attack on Pearl Harbor, stress the dominant orientation. Internally, moreover, Hoover's "chicken in every pot" and Roosevelt's "forgotten man" were both appeals to the egalitarian and democratic American ethos. They were in neither case conceived by their political consumers as other than Americanism. They were not for export. They were not obviously dependent on our own world power, nor on world conditions. These last could at most upset our own achievement. They were not an inevitable part of our success or failure nor a necessary setting for our internal enterprise.

World War II was long and arduous. In its course the United States emerged conspicuous as a dominant power. A large part of the world became manifestly dependent on its leadership and assistance for reconstruction and stability. For a moment, a radical change in American thinking seemed probable. Isolationism appeared destined to disappear through a United Nations, where this country would have its achievements acknowledged as a basis and model for creative peace. Unfortunately, even before the Charter was complete, the potentialities for bipolar organization of that world were clear to the perceptive observer, and actual bipolar conflict was soon to follow. As the conflict deepened, it became evident that this country had little chance either to impose its model and enjoy its leadership undisturbed or to retire unconcernedly to cultivate its garden, already long neglected. Kings and courts were gone, the major fascist dictatorships had been liquidated. But a new totalitarianism constituted a novel, and more mysterious, threat to either self-cultivation or hegemony. It was even more broadly continental than ourselves. It was, moreover, committed in theory to ideological world conquest and, in practice, to threatening expansion in an age of interconnectedness and atomic energy. It was doubly disturbing because it challenged the self-confidence of the New World with a still newer doctrine. It could not be treated as an exasperatingly decadent annoyance which was yet the source, and sometime the inspiration, of our own adventure. It was possessed of the dual desire to preserve its own adventure and to make the world conform to its mode. Its insecure boastfulness and aggressive sense of superiority and power were frighteningly reminiscent, for all the differences, of our own more genial ambivalence.

The impossibility of isolation

Meanwhile Western Europe was the sick man of America, as Turkey had once been of Europe. A bulwark and outpost, it seemed to be also a bottomless well. It drained our resources for its defense and reconstruction without apparent major revival of its economy or restoration of morale. The result was inflation here at home, high taxes, and the prevention of full enjoyment of the American way of life, even under conditions of full employment. Despite its own failure to achieve internally the promise of the "more abundant life," as Hoover had once phrased the aspiration for this country, Russia, the new enemy, seemed likely to invalidate the American claim to superior well-being by reason of the costs of meeting its international challenge to our interests and our leadership. Simultaneously it appeared to threaten America's internal freedom and welfare. Both by its expansionist drive elsewhere and by its encouragement of subversive activities here, it imposed on us the necessity for strong peacetime controls. Likewise, it enforced a drainage of American resources to bolster—or to re-create—our military defenses.

At this juncture, isolationism revived in a new form, as a consequence of exasperation and despair. To win the consent and stimulate the creative energies of other peoples after the American pattern seemed to many an impossible and ruinous adventure. Our difficulties

made plausible the demands by professed patriots that traditional liberties be curtailed and that alien techniques of curbing expression be
imposed in the name of national security. The new insularism sought to
minimize aid, in the name of economy, or to eliminate it; as it sought
to maximize our own productivity. It aimed to make ourselves—upon
whom alone we could surely rely—solely responsible for our own defense. Thus, more would be produced at less cost. A hopeless adventure,
whose end could be attrition of our own resources and powers and the
triumph of our opponents, would be avoided. This whole position, which
constituted a doctrine of defensive isolation or of independence from
interdependence, was given persuasive buttressing by a new theory of
military strategy. This continent was effectively defensible against air
attack, provided all efforts were concentrated on that task, and concepts of wider frontiers to patrol and defend were firmly abandoned.

The unexpectedly long and seemingly fruitless struggle in Korea,
and the fear of a war with China, re-inforced this recessive current
in thinking. But its main strength was an economic doctrine, with a
purportedly ethical foundation. Our moralistic individualism judged
Europe adversely for its failure to reveal the strengths and energies
of this country and, despite changes in political institutions, to emulate
successfully our own way of life.

The course of modern history makes such a program both anachronistic and ultimately impotent to secure its own professed purpose. For
that history is dominated by an industrialism born in Europe. It matured
here, where it has proved an effective means to satisfy the long-lived
human aspiration to the material bases of the good life. At the beginning of the period the United States, begotten in the age of the maturing
European nation-state, and itself the product of the expansion of Europe, properly adopted insulationism as a technique for equality of status
in that world. Insulationism as a course for the infant Republic was
sensible as a means to protect a novel adventure whose contours and
consequences were but dimly glimpsed. Under that policy the United
States became the first continent-wide, constitutional, industrial state.
As such, it achieved leadership in an interconnected global order dom-

inated increasingly by continental and subcontinental states. To their pattern Europe itself is even today endeavoring to conform, with enormous stress and strain.

As America achieved international power it developed an isolationism based largely on a desire to escape the shackles, and reject the commitments, of the old and untransformed Europe. Aware of its differences and its promise, it failed to perceive fully the newly emerging pattern, which renders the old Europe largely meaningless and unimportant. As the envied leader in a world of subcontinent states, some more populous but less developed or endowed than itself, the United States is in the long run denied the possibility of lasting isolation, which is incompatible with adequate self-defense and consequent security in differential well-being. Its alternative is to offer promise to others by assistance to them in the emulation of its ways and standards, or to confront the hostility of continent-states allied in opposition to its unshared and selfishly defended privileges. Moreover, like other pioneers such as England, it cannot hope everlastingly to enjoy the rewards of pioneering, in a world where others can imitate. It can only seek the prestige of a statesman-like leadership which persuades others of superior promise for their lives through following its path. By stressing probable gains to its friends and by making clear its own sympathetic mutuality, the United States must endeavor to persuade the less fortunate peoples of the world to moderate their envy as they strive slowly to bridge the gap.

Isolationism is today useless as an effective defense. It is a psychological barrier to responsible leadership. It contains an obvious warning to others that they should be cautious in putting their reliance or their hopes on the American people. Consequently, it brings no conceivable gains as policy. Certainly, a lack of confidence on the part of others in a nation which ought through position to instill confidence cannot be accounted gain. Nor can we afford a belated childhood wherein we ourselves continuously seek assurance and psychological support. A world power which shirks or shrinks from responsibility and leadership in its world will in time stand alone. Moreover, soon or late, it is apt to fall in isolation, unloved and unlamented.

III

Hindrances to policy: Individualism and legalism

Isolationism is a corruption of a once internally useful and internationally harmless search for conditions of national self-development. Its claim to historical justification rests on an undue stress on forms. Its advocates neglect changing world conditions and the modern changes in America's power position. They fail to realize that these changes make insulation itself irrelevant to the present national interests of the United States, which must be conceived as essentially international. Isolationists have failed to learn the lesson or achieve the hard-won wisdom of the late Senator Vandenberg. In the short run, indeed, it might prove possible to defend this country—and so to preserve its privileged standard of living—by a coherent military policy devoted exclusively to that end. Such isolationism, however, would beget envy and resentment abroad and would prove morally corrupting at home. Moreover, in the long run the United States could retain neither independence nor superior living standards in a world increasingly united against it by its own deliberate withdrawal and unconcern.

At the moment pure isolationism seems to be recessive. It is not, however, dead. It thrives, indeed, in modified and impure forms which deceptively hide or cast doubts on its continued reality. For they seem to contradict its essence, since they involve an admission that, as prerequisite or concomitant of effective isolation, assistance to Europe or intervention in the Far East are inescapably necessary. Such admissions are indeed denials of the adequacy of isolationism and make conspicuous the inevitability of our active involvement in global affairs. Thereby they glaringly reveal the difference in circumstances and the divergences in American doctrine between the present and the national past. But they involve no psychological contradiction: the acceptance of limited responsibilities elsewhere as a foundation for an ultimate, if not an immediately practical, isolationism is needful to inner comfort and to persuasiveness; for purposes of political practice and appealing prophecy, it is impossible to be a complete ostrich. Nevertheless, the admission of current needs, in which the term "beyond our control" is also not foreseeable, surely raises a legitimate suspicion that the ideal itself is at best utopian myth.

For the moment, the isolationist, his back to the wall and his eyes on a never-never land, is prepared to support programs of limited commitments and hard-boiled assistance to others devised to involve a minimal present cost to ourselves and to produce in due course the possibility of our full withdrawal. Such a proposed policy has been revealed in various congressional debates on aid to Europe. It might be described as an attempt to make the world safe for American retreat from it.

Secondly, in relation to the Far East, isolationists tend to a more aggressive program, which is designed to contain and combat the U.S.S.R. Yet here again their dominant objective is to secure safe isolation. Their formal profession is a concern for Chinese independence. But their actual support for the Nationalist cause of Chiang rests on a desire to have that safety obtained at minimum initial American cost, and without continued American responsibility or involvement. That desire is supplemented by the remains of an Open Door policy: China must be

made safe and available for private American investment and enterprise; and Americans must be free to conduct their business in that
country without direct responsibility for any broader public policy or
costs.

This last position is, in turn, a special application of a more general
doctrine, whose essence is that Americans must be free to venture in the
world. Government must protect that freedom. It must not go further
in an attempt to secure for us an acknowledged position of public leadership and responsibility in a world-wide political economy. Nor must
it expect its nationals abroad to be altruistically or politically concerned
with the wealth and welfare of other peoples. An indirect isolationism
is therefore buttressed by a specific theory of individual enterprise in
the realm of international economics. That theory is itself a derivative
of individualism, which is one of the basic elements in the American
tradition. But individualism as a hindrance to effective foreign policy
requires independent examination.

Roots of individualism

Individualism has been a central theme of the American adventure
almost since the Colonial beginnings. The Puritans' opposition to this-
worldly distinctions and to monarchical power and glory themselves
provided a poor long-term basis for their own attempted resistance to
demands for individual freedom. Despite their theocratic concept of
the restrictive ordering of earthly life, they could not completely escape
the individualistic implications of that Reformation which had begotten them. The more radical insights of Protestantism worked together
with a free wilderness and resultant opportunities to escape confin-
ing communities and concepts in such a way as to undermine the
would-be closed society of the Puritans and to combat their aristocratic
concept of the elect. The joint consequences of these developments were
the assertion of common human dignity, the proclamation of equality

of opportunity, and support of men's claim for freedom to use their creative energies without needless let or hindrance.

Such ideas comprise the essence of the doctrine of individualism. The search to embody them in institutions and behaviors has constituted a sustained thrust in that commitment to unrelenting and energetic activity so characteristic of American life. That search is historically the moral core of our public life. It ought to remain so for the future. Individualism is the root of our anti-statist tradition. It is the foundation of our social and political pluralism; our reliance on the free creation and activity of voluntary groups either for direct action or for influence on policy in order to meet needs not to be satisfied by the unaided individual. It is the basis of our past opposition to a narrowly political and monistic concept of this nation's interest. Yet the consequence of such individualistic opposition has been a profound ambiguity in our attitude to foreign affairs, where we have found it extraordinarily difficult to propound coherent concepts of national interest consistently with defense of the rights claimed for the individual at home and abroad. Likewise, we have found it hard to reconcile the primacy of America interest with the implication that individualism is a way of life of universal applicability, to be guaranteed to all our own citizens, and to be available to others without restriction, were they but willing to follow it. Initially, indeed, our concept of national interest and our insistence on individual freedom—abroad no less than at home—involved no inner conflicts. They led to no radical incompatibilities between internal well-being and international security. But today their outcome is internal contradiction in thought, insoluble tension in feeling, and irresolution and incoherence in policy.

At the outset of our venture as a free and independent people, the Hamiltonian system had happily harmonized national interest and the freedom of individual venturing. From the beginning, the protection of infant industries and encouragement of manufacturers were inimical to the dominance and exclusive development of a purely agrarian individualism. The Hamiltonian system avowedly equalized opportunities for the use of different talents and promoted varied enterprises. It led to the satisfaction of more individuals and groups through the use of their respective energies and abilities. It created a more balanced economy. It provided the roots of national strength by deliverance from the dangers of colonialism. It produced a happy harmony between individual self-interest and national welfare and strength. By government policy, Hamilton had set the conditions for the working of a hidden hand. Yet, as Jefferson foresaw and John Taylor of Caroline early demonstrated, the development of that system necessarily raised questions as to who should be privileged to venture where, in what channels, and how far. The lasting American conflict of the two individualisms, agrarian and industrial, was inescapable, as was the inequality in their power consequent on the nature of industrial technology and organization. In the long run, moreover, these questions were to create central issues of foreign policy. But at the moment, England was the dominant industrializing power and sought markets to which it might export its new manufactures. The United States, Hamilton saw, had to strive to escape economic colonial status. His successful system unified domestic and foreign policy, as it harnessed individualism to national interest. For a long time to come, it maximized the total range of opportunity available to Americans in a diversified economy, ultimately continent-wide. The significance of that achievement was not lessened by the fact that tariffs were hampering to the development of some enterprises; nor by the nature of tariff bargains and of the pressures creating protective duties. Certainly the national system of Henry Clay, whatever its biases, furthered rather than combatted the Hamiltonian concept of the compatibility of individual enterprise and national interest. Likewise, it strengthened the whole idea of freedom of opportunity for Americans in their own country. Insulationism and individualism were in this context parts of a single whole.

Later this country achieved industrial dominance. Infant industries grew into giants. Their right to tariff protection then became a selfish privilege. Tariffs ceased to be of service to the whole nation, or manifestly in the interests of its security and power. Likewise, they ceased to guarantee equal opportunity for different individuals and interests within the nation. Nor were they needed any longer as a protection against more powerful or industrially advanced European nations or as insurance against colonial status. Instead, the protective tariff came to constitute a paramount factor in the transformation from an understandable desire for self-sufficiency into isolationism. The American individual and the American people moved from an insurance of equality of opportunity toward a system of special consideration for Americans only and to the safeguarding against others of our own higher standards of living. By the twentieth century, this development meant something more than, and something different from, inequalities between persons here and elsewhere. Older industrial nations either suffered decreased industrial efficiency vis-à-vis ourselves, or they were unable to use their full productive capacity without access to our markets. Meanwhile, American investors aided other nations, including those not hitherto industrialized, in the development of their own capital goods equipment. The latter thereupon needed markets both to protect their own minimum well-being and political stability and to repay those whose money had helped make possible their conditioning and imperative economic environment. The American tariff system consequently became a threat to their own welfare. It constituted an impediment to the effective use and sustained operation of the equipment with which we had so largely supplied them. It prevented full enjoyment of those higher standards of living which industrialization was supposed to bring. With or without our aid, many other peoples had come to possess productive capacity beyond the needs of their home market and wanted access to ours, which was so vast in area and population, and seemed to provide an inexhaustible demand for goods and services. Regardless of the soundness of their position, the leaders of peoples whom we had aided in industrial development felt that we had misled them as to the promise of industrialism; and that our tariff system was unneighborly since the infant industries argument no longer applied.

The second part of the Hamiltonian system had been an acceptance of free trade as unhampered access to unrestricted markets outside our boundaries, and a doctrine of individual enterprise by Americans in the world. Such enterprise was to be furthered by diplomacy and by the use of the instrumentalities of government to gain respect for the free movement and free action of its citizens abroad. Individualism had its own ethic of unrestrictive order, of stable peace, and of legally secured rights. In particular, it asserted claims to equality of persons abroad, on the high seas, or in areas not in origin parts of the Western states system.

In one sense such doctrine was properly the obverse of protectionism at home. The purpose of the latter had been equality of effective opportunity for all persons here to embark on such undertakings as they desired. Subsequently, as a result of a policy of free immigration to this country, later supplemented by the offer of free land under the Homestead Acts, it had made a chance to share in this country's development available to all Europeans who could come. Beyond our boundaries the fundamental American concept was one of freedom and opportunity for individual persons. The role of the United States government was to secure the relevant conditions as far as its own nationals were concerned. On this general thesis a major element in our foreign policy gains coherence: from our concern to dispose of the Barbary pirates, through our concepts of neutrality and freedom of the seas, to John Hay's Open Door, the root idea is the right of Americans and, on occasion and by necessary extension, of others to undisturbed movement and use of their energies in the world.

The political ideas, as well as the economic expansion, which followed the Civil War reinforced, rather than diminished, commitment to this concept. For the nationalist doctrines begotten of that conflict were not conceived in terms of the state as an activating force, far less as director and master. Rather, they were buttresses of individual adventuring and individualistic competitive enterprise. The nation was the locus of the release of personal energies, as Social Darwinism was the road by which those energies might achieve the collective manifest destiny. Nor did the importation of German ideas of state and sovereignty change this situation: those ideas were always reconciled, by whatever logic, with the supposed English view of liberty. In the economic sphere that view was, moreover, identified with dominantly American ideas of rights of opportunity and of acquisition. Whatever the possible conflicts between those rights in practice, they rested on the same fundamental presuppositions. Here again, our tariff manners are revealing: tariffs were products of interest conflicts, with each interest concerned with its particular enterprise, and scarcely conscious of the international repercussions of its own defense and promotion. The deliberate devising of tariffs as instruments of national policy for dominantly international power purposes was not the American way. The European practice of tariff wars between states was scarcely imagined by the pressure groups in whose interests and on whose claimed needs tariffs were argued and bargained in Congress. Retrospect may indeed reveal the interconnections of our own and European tariff barriers. But those connections rest on the response of particular American industries to European actions which affected our markets, and especially our home market, rather than on a concerted national policy which deliberately tied our own national economic strength to a unified national political power, of which government was the deliberate instrument.

No doubt in European countries, not less than here, particular interests exerted pressures behind the scenes. There, too, such pressures shaped the contours and helped to determine the height of tariff walls. But there the public defense of tariffs was professedly on grounds of national political interest. There business itself was more consciously political, and the ruling classes, economic and political, were much more integrated. Europe did not share America's extreme antimonopolistic professions. Its developing cartels were accepted as in the national interest. By contrast, American corporations thought of themselves as individual persons not affected with a public interest. Government was their limited instrument. They were not its servants, nor yet its deliberate allies. Certainly our business interests did not conceive that their appeal to government for protection was in truth an acknowledgment that they had a responsible role in the conduct of foreign policy. They were hindered from developing such an attitude, because they looked primarily to the home market for their strength and envisaged tariff barriers in the light of the insulationist tradition. Moreover, the distance from Europe and the lack of direct involvement in its national system and imperial rivalries seemed to warrant this peculiarly American outlook.

What is significant, however, is that psychologically the individualisms of our internal expansion reinforced the view that it was the American individual's right freely to carry on his enterprises abroad, as well as himself to move about unrestrictedly. He must not be prevented from venturing and bargaining where he willed and could. Rather, he must be positively assured opportunity to move and conduct business anywhere in the world without fear, favor, or discrimination. Indeed, save for a small critical minority, the change from insulationism to isolationism brought no recognition that our own abandonment of what had in truth been a partly Open Door at home might justly diminish our claims to free venturing beyond our boundaries. In some sense, too, the failure to develop a new attitude was intelligible. Until after World War I, movement to and in Europe was fairly free. Even the subsequent boundary controls and the new exasperation of passports and visas, as well as of baggage inspections which had hitherto been a nuisance only to limited groups of returning travelers at our own borders, hardly affected the growing hordes of Americans abroad, so welcome for the dollars they brought with them.

Moreover, the growth of the big corporation, or of the huge personal industry or bank, had little or no effect in bringing about a different viewpoint. Rather, such growth reinforced the prevailing view, especially since corporations, who had been made persons under the Fourteenth Amendment, took on the protective coloration of individualism. First from conscious interest, and then by habit and sincere conviction, corporations came to regard themselves as in fact proper parts of the individualist pattern. What is more, they did venture abroad and were largely welcome. In due course they came to deal with governments on terms of near-equality. As a consequence, they looked on sovereign states as parties to private contracts, equals in law and right. In their dealings with governments, they applied the ethics of business transactions. Moreover, they did so without any sense of impropriety or incongruity.

Controls and individualism

The early developments of internal regulation and control, though they increased the powers of the federal government and were precursors of thoroughgoing public-welfare government, in no sense changed the picture. For their dominant intent was to purify individualism. They sought to make equality of opportunity real. They strove to eliminate unfair practices by monopolies, or corporations in pursuit of monopoly. Those developments culminated in the first term of Woodrow Wilson, the very title of whose program, The New Freedom, is testimony to that intent and orientation. What is more, the rallying cry of his second campaign was in truth an appeal to enjoy the American way of life, thus purified, without shock or disturbance by the conflict consequent on the national rivalries and state ambitions of Europe, which appeared so alien to American folkways.

Our subsequent involvement and participation in that conflict was no doubt based partly on sympathy with England and on the special heritage we shared with her. But it had as its dominant cause a somewhat perverted, selfish, and morally isolationist concept of an American right to undisturbed individual movement and enterprise. Such a right necessitated—and from the American viewpoint warranted—unchallenged acceptance of our political-social attachments in the warring world and on the high seas, which were major battlegrounds. The assertion of this right was perverse only because the conditions of warfare and the scale of organization had changed: the practices which had marked the Napoleonic Wars were now extended across the Atlantic, though the parties were different. In essence the American plea was business as usual. We asserted the undisputed right of the nation to enjoy neutrality and of the individual to profit from it. Our own bias in the use of neutrality and its unequal impact on the contending parties were in our view irrelevant to judgment of their behavior. Our attitudes and activities did not justify their questioning or forcible denial of the right itself. Rather, our sympathies and our moral convictions of the just claims to respect due civilians, especially when neutral, allowed us to muster effective indignation against Germany. The attitude was plainly revealed in American reactions to the sinking of the *Lusitania*, which England effectively exploited. In the course of time it allowed us to enter the war in defense of an American individualism. That defense was soon transformed into a crusade to make the world safe for democracy.

Participation itself, however, meant new controls. The needs of modern war speedily demonstrated that the American tradition of modified volunteering was not able to create an adequate army. In a mass society habituated to disciplined organization, it was even an irrelevance. Thus, the very conditions for our participation in the war, as a means to defend an individualistic concept of freedom and neutral rights, resulted in at least temporary rejections of individualism, as well as abandonment of isolationism. The consequence was a revelation of the imperfect harmony of the two parts of American policy. Indeed, a serious question arose as to whether, for the future, American politics and policy could be lastingly integrated or effectively conducted on the ancient premises. The favorable balance of trade then acquired was to give the answer. Subsequent private investment in Europe, probably inescapable even if in actual course unwise, reinforced the point. Yet the lesson is still far from learned.

American individualism and the League of Nations

For all his noble aspiration towards a better world order, towards lasting peace, towards democracy and human dignity, Woodrow Wilson himself certainly did not give the needed answer. In historical perspective, the League of Nations, engineered by him, by Smuts, and by Robert Cecil, was a step in the evolution of international thought and in its slow institutionalization. It was the continuation of a trend which runs from late medieval times through Rousseau and Kant to the Concert of Europe and the Hague Conferences. But that League, especially as it was fitted into the peace settlements, was also a continuation with modified technique of the nation-states system of Europe—"A timid compromise between nationalism and internationalism." Wilson paid dearly to get it, on the illusion that it would usher in a new and braver world. Yet actually he was continuing our initial adherence to the old European system. He was doing so, however, without the initial intent, which was participation to insure us against disturbance by European powers. Such an objective was by that time in truth an irrelevance. The perversion of insulationism, the isolationism proffered by his opponents, stressed the other element in our tradition and was at least equally irrelevant. The two jointly prophesied the need for fundamental reorientation if the American vision was to be lastingly protected at home and preserved in its appeal abroad.

Yet the failure of Wilson's design was not due merely to his acceptance of an antiquated nation-state system in a continental world. It flowed even more from his very defense of individualism. The insulation and protection of the new freedom and effective championing of the American interest as individualistic freedom in the world were indeed fundamentally incompatible, whatever their apparent unity. Yet Wilson was in intent consistent, as he was striving to be true to both elements in our tradition. The New Freedom was purified individualism at home. Participation in the War and the creation of the League were means to assure individualist freedom in the world at large, after the American pattern. In an age when the Hamiltonian argument had become irrelevant, Wilson was no high-tariff man. Beyond our borders, he was a clear defender of basic human rights in general, and of free enterprise as free trade and unhampered individual initiative in world markets in particular. He did not believe that the organization of nations committed to concepts of national power through the monistic state was incompatible with the free venturing of individuals in international trade. Nevertheless a policy devised to further the latter was rendered doubly irrelevant by the commitment of many nations to public social welfare programs which necessitated increased governmental functions. Moreover, monopolistic cartels, whether they dominated governments or were their economic instruments in international affairs, in practice reinforced a statist approach, rather than combatted it. Here again Wilson's opponents revealed a clearer insight: the protection of the traditional American individualism at home, and avoidance of statism, must involve a return to normalcy, of which abstention from the League was an essential part.

The League of Nations and the practice of international free trade and free movement of persons about the world were by no means corollaries. Nevertheless, the United States could not isolate itself for the pursuit of individualistic enterprise at home without regard to the rest of the world. Nor could it, on the one hand, count on freedom for its enterprising citizens beyond its boundaries or, on the other, be unaffected in its power and policies by what they chanced to do. In the era of Coolidge prosperity America became, it is true, the world's chief single banker, even though the total of European investment remained greater, and England continued to profit from its habitual money-market skill. The vast postwar demand for American capital abroad appeared to make private international investment an easy matter, which did not require any League organization or governmental assistance or control. Rather, the economic motivations of American investment houses enabled them to utilize favorable conditions to further and strengthen the old doctrine of individualism beyond our borders. Yet the long-lived headache of war debts and reparations was a public, political, and private investment question. Settlement of these issues was fundamental to the confidence of our own would-be and actual investors. But such settlement could not be divorced from the actions and relations of the governments involved: in origin and content, the problems were both public and international. Demand for loans abroad and supply of funds at home were both present. Nevertheless, the conclusion of bargains between private parties, or between these and public authorities, depended on government actions—on commitments, policies, and guarantees. Our own government was eager to create conditions which would beget public confidence. On the theory of political economy then prevailing, it was eager to do so in the very service of such investment interests. But it also recognized its own political interest in stability and stabilization elsewhere.

American leadership in the making of the Dawes and Young plans, American participation in international economic conferences, American adherence to various League organizations and activities—including the International Labor Organization—were all pragmatic attempts to give recognition to the inescapable need of relating public action and private individual enterprise in the international field. The traditional individualism had to be preserved as American policy, and a statist nationalism had to be avoided. But under the changed conditions these results could be attained only by new techniques which utilized governmental power and the skills of statesmen. Yet the techniques devised proved inadequate. They did not succeed in developing a coherent formulation and defense of American national interest as international.

The reasons for our failure were, no doubt, complex. But they included our rather naïve and moralistic aspirations to internationalism or cosmopolitanism. These worked at cross-purposes with any attempt at a genuine welding of political instrumentality and individualistic enterprise. They included, secondly, our acceptance, ready or reluctant, of European doctrines of sovereignty and nationalism as usual. We were thereby prevented from imposing effective conditions and controls over the use of loans. That situation was, indeed, repeated later with equally disastrous consequences in dealings with Nationalist China. In both instances inadequate accustomedness to leadership on our part was no doubt largely to blame.

Lastly, our failure rested in part on the inability of our own enterprisers and investment houses to recognize that their business was affected with a public interest. Our business and financial leaders did not perceive that they themselves were also instruments of policy. They did not acknowledge that they were to a large degree responsible for the furtherance and protection of the national interest. Rather, as enterprisers they followed the motivation of anticipated profits. They insisted that government ought to be—and they saw to it that it was—directed by their advice. It must use its power and influence to create conditions of political security serviceable to their ventures. Nevertheless they themselves followed no larger and statesmanlike motivation.

They were seemingly incapable of broad political, rather than narrow and short-term economic, judgment. Nor did they perceive that political assistance imposed a reciprocal responsibility on them. They did not recognize or acknowledge that they had no right so to venture as to undermine the effectiveness of that public action which they had themselves solicited and espoused.

No doubt these last attitudes were neither fully conscious nor deliberately irresponsible. They rested, indeed, to a large extent on long-lived assumptions about the nature and prerogatives of private enterprise. They also followed, at least in part, from a sharing in a more general optimism, to whose creation they had contributed. Further, they betokened a failure to realize that Europe, as well as Latin America, was not the United States. Those countries did not enjoy the potentialities which within our boundaries had warranted optimism, and on balance had justified even rashly expansionist enterprise at home.

Individualism and the depression

Our own stock-market collapse and the subsequent failure of the Kreditanstalt in Vienna signaled depression at home and abroad. That depression was for the United States a ruthless commentary on its inability to make a coherent policy juxtaposing isolationism, internationalism, and individualism. Unhappily, it also signified the inadequate adaptation of the American tradition. Changed circumstances had not yet created a system or a technique for the harmonizing of private and public interest. To achieve that end necessitated a wide extension of government controls over both the internal and the international enterprise of American business. In particular, it made controls over the latter essential in order to further the nation's own political-economic interest. The whole problem of politics became one of how to achieve the needful compounding of private and public, as well as of internal and international, interests without lapsing into statism. It was necessary to preserve the essential pluralism and scope for group and individual energies which were the superiority of the American way of life. Yet it was necessary to prevent anarchy and to overcome that absence of business answerability which had earlier been relatively harmless and had indeed constituted a major condition for creative use of energies.

The New Deal initially embodied some promise of a useful change in orientation, based on informed insight. For it was essentially a rescue operation: national government undertook positive action to overcome the disastrous consequences of behaviors consequent on inadequate analysis and erroneous doctrine. Its program involved, indeed, both restrictions and promotion to refine and reform our mores and our institutions. But its object was to restore as a going concern the social-economic system of American enterprise. It was properly critical of the abuses and miscalculations of business, whether at home or in its foreign investment policies. For these had resulted in the disastrous debacle. It was impatient with the prior policies of the Hoover regime, which had deemed the Reconstruction Finance Corporation a sufficient restorative. Therefore it aimed, by a series of interrelated measures, to start up again the wheels of industry and to revivify the agrarian segment of our society. It sought to do so, too, by soliciting the co-operation of the interests involved, as the ill-fated National Industrial Recovery Act attests. Consequently, at the start it was recognized by many leaders of the business community as necessary and serviceable to that individualism which they held fundamental. For a moment a re-emerging concept of responsible trusteeship, almost lost since the Civil War, seemed possible. Some evidence, indeed, suggested that leaders in the business world, shocked by their own and others' misfortunes, were coming to develop a statesmanlike attitude. They would, it was hoped, broaden their motivations. There might then emerge a pattern of co-partnership between social-economic and political leadership. Such a pattern could well constitute a preservative of freedom from statism. Yet it would utilize the instrumentalities of government as a technique for adjustments between public and private interests, between government and particular interest groups. Such adjustments would result in an imperfect but dynamic harmony consequent on deliberate action undertaken in the service of the complex American society.

The honeymoon was, however, brief. The new governmental activity had at the start involved a proper and limited restoration of the statesman's calling and a renewed insistence on public responsibility and public service. But it soon resulted in an expansion of governmental functions considerably in excess of what was needed to release the energies of the productive parts of the community. The New Deal program moved far beyond what was necessitated by business abuses and by denials of equality of opportunity. It became at many points a hindrance rather than a help to socially useful creative effort. The consequence was widespread fear that we would become subjects of a bureaucratic state. The danger was real, though not immediate. No doubt the fear was exaggerated by unfamiliarity and unaccustomedness to widespread governmental function. Moreover, the threat itself might have been met by a positive program of restraints and controls on government. But a major part of the business community had long been conditioned to the idea of its own primacy. It was convinced of the sufficiency of its own economic and power motivations. Hence it regarded the whole New Deal operation as temporary and abnormal. Therefore, once some degree of confidence was re-established, it sought another return to normalcy, though it was to suffer repeated frustrations. Its inherited doctrine of stabilized finance, part of the mores of individualism which it applied uncritically to public affairs, increased its drive to escape from the confines of government.

In any event, there arose a deep conflict between those who saw individualism as the root concept of the American adventure and those for whom a positive concern for social welfare was the overriding criterion in the conduct of public life. The consequence of their political irreconcilability during this period was the destruction of a germinating dynamic conservatism. Such a conservatism was nevertheless essential for the reinterpretation of the basic American tradition to meet contemporary conditions. A progressive Toryism had been within reach, embodying a combination of *noblesse oblige* and enlightened self-interest on the part of business leaders who felt a new responsibility and accepted the justice of mass demands for greater security and a greater share in the rewards of an industrial order. Under its aegis, individual freedom and public responsibility could have been reconciled and harnessed in the service of American society as a whole. But the dogmas of nineteenth-century individualism, reinforced by a more ancient American heritage, proved too strong. Classical liberalism remained the essence of professed American conservatism. A genuinely conservationist conservatism failed to emerge.

That failure resulted in sustained dichotomy within our political society. Henceforth our politics was marked by increasing acrimony. The bitterness was disastrous both for internal and for international politics, however great the value for democratic institutions of genuine two-party fights. For mutual recriminations prevented the full and cheerful acceptance of the doctrine of co-partnership of government and the social economic order, today the essential alternative to statist planning. The recognition that big government was a useful and useable instrument was denied by one major segment of our society. The values of free individual and group enterprise were seriously questioned by the other.

The failure likewise prevented the necessary integration of domestic programs and international policies as a coherent expression of the national interest: the vision of the United States as a co-organic society incapable of isolation and obligated to leadership was at best seriously blurred. The opposition to such a design by doctrinaire individualists at home made difficult an appropriate redefinition of national interest in the service of an American international policy and of America's actual position. It re-emphasized the older theory of uncontrolled individualistic venturing, in a world where that viewpoint was no longer serviceable or safe.

Within government itself, the conflict between Wilsonian patterns and a concept of America's carefully compounded and coherently implemented international interest had already occurred. It had destroyed the initial New Deal harmony. It had contributed to the wrecking of the London International Economic Conference. The depression itself had indeed led to a greater recognition of economic interdependence in at least the Western world. Such awareness diminished overt isolationist opposition to participation in efforts to revive world trade and restore the functioning of other economies. But the very urgency of internal problems and the common distress at unfortunate investment abroad worked in the other direction. The failure by some of the official family to perceive the irrelevance of earlier concepts of international enterprise, together with enforced concentration on domestic problems, prevented an effective extension of the initial New Deal statecraft to the whole realm of policy.

Individualism, isolationism, and world conflict

The end of the brief honeymoon of government and business meant in turn a revival of isolationist thinking. That revival was unemphatic only because the general orientation of our people was internal. Willingness to venture abroad slowly and cautiously revived. But the doctrine of controls over venturing in the name of national interest was not accepted. We did not consciously endeavor to promote international policies favorable to our well-being at home and to the extension abroad of American institutional patterns. Our government did not consistently undertake to prevent endeavors which might prove politically harmful, however economically rewarding. Such courses were, indeed, publicly advocated only with hesitancy, uncertainly and unsystematically.

Nevertheless, the growth of executive power in the making of reciprocal trade agreements was a radical departure from the concept of interest-bargained tariffs. It moved towards the idea of the nation's collective political-economic interest as international. Subsequently, too, as World War II came in Europe and crisis grew in the Far East, the system of export licenses and of increasingly stringent controls on the movements of our own nationals evidenced a growing awareness of the need to circumscribe the claims of individuals to freedom in their venturings abroad for the very sake of protection and furtherance of a collective interest. In a different and more direct way, our aid to and deals with Great Britain prior to our own entry into the war also revealed our recognition of the inescapable primacy of the political, and of the necessity to define the national interest as a joint and international one.

Nevertheless, it proved genuinely difficult to prepare the public mind for participation in a conflict in Europe, even though the result of that conflict would clearly affect our destiny. Indeed, only with Pearl Harbor was the die cast. That difficulty is testimony to the prevalence in the country of both isolationist and individualistic attitudes which opposed involvement beyond our borders and revealed deep fearfulness of further interferences with normal freedoms. The debate over preparedness through compulsory military training is here additional supporting evidence. Once we were involved in the war, however, thoroughgoing controls over the economy, including manpower controls, were accepted with reasonably good grace. What is more, they were made effective in the main by the co-operation and voluntary compliance, despite grumblings, of the various interests affected, including the rationed public.

Bureaucracy was necessarily omnipresent, and frequently it was awkward and inept. Nevertheless, at several key points long participation by representatives of specific interests or of the public at large insured against a purely centralized statism. Moreover, given the normal dominance of government in wartime, the actual conduct of affairs remained much closer than might have been anticipated to that co-partnership which is the proper corollary of a societal concept of national interest.

Yet, the war once ended, it proved impossible for government to resist the individualistic demand for a return to a second normalcy. Public pressure forced the rapid removal of controls and the speedy return home and to civilian life of soldiers abroad. Demands for decontrol were no doubt to a considerable degree the consequence of the individualistic preconceptions and motivations of enterprisers. Insistence on demobilization rested on somewhat curious sentimentalities and moralities which pointed to the survival of an underlying geographical and cultural isolationism. Both alike were testimony to a more widespread antistatism and to the generic character of American individualism: neither economy nor persons should be under the orders of government if such a course were in any way avoidable without danger of disaster. The subsequent fear of militarism through major participation of military men in policy-making was likewise an indication of our individualism. For such opposition went beyond traditional concern for civilian supremacy and provided a technique wherewith to attack the expanded range of governmental power and function.

The fear of statism and the desire to preserve individual freedom were by no means evil in themselves. They rested on the lasting American insight and aspiration, as they embodied an ethically sound critical judgment. But subsequent dislocations, the necessity of a rapid return to controls, owing to increasing bipolar conflict, and the serious weakening of our power and prestige in Europe are indications of the inadequacy of an older individualism. Our worried, frenzied, and costly undertaking of a needed military preparedness further emphasized that inadequacy. In many areas traditional individualism had already become more a creed than a practice. Nevertheless, the assumptions underlying the creed—powerful even when impracticable—constitute false criteria for the conduct of domestic and foreign policy, today inescapably intertwined: they do not fit modern conditions. In particular, they are not consonant with our own position of leadership and the clear international character of our present national interest. They are likewise evidence of our signal failure lastingly to develop our own proper alternative to statism, namely, collaboration of public authority and private interests based on statesmanlike awareness of an overriding general welfare.

The failure is indeed only partial. It involves the privation of a possible good. It does not consist in the presence of individualism and attachment to the primacy of the person. Indeed, our determination that men's energies shall not be confined and directed by the state according to the pleasure of elected persons or at the behest of bureaucrats is itself valuable. Rather, failure arises from our conceiving the state as enemy, and not as useful and necessary instrument in the formulation and pursuit of that general welfare. For such welfare constitutes the proper American criterion both for governmental action and for individual freedom. The corollary of our error in thought and feeling is an inability on the part of the leaders in our social-economic order to develop an overriding sense of statesmanship. Such failure must sooner or later prove fatal to genuine individualism, which can remain vital only while it is grounded in moral principle. Inadequately enlightened individualism and the absence of a clear concept of the duty of statesmanship result in our lack of appropriate and adequate means to correct the excesses of faith in business leadership of the Republic. We still find it hard to persuade leaders in economic life that the pursuit of business as usual from their viewpoint, under strictly economic or corporate organizational motivations, is not a sufficient performance of their obligation as enterprisers and as citizens. Whatever its past values in developing a continent, that viewpoint is today too narrow. Recently the heritage of an isolating and competitive individualism has stood in the way of an effective dynamic conservatism. It has impeded us in our search to discover concepts of citizenship and leadership adequate for our time.

Individualism and American postwar leadership

The central consequence of World War II was that the United States became conspicuously and by common acknowledgment the leader of the Western world. Indeed, for much of Asia not less than for Europe, its generic way of life offered the sole alternative to Communism, as its aid in the promotion and preservation of nontotalitarian institutions was a major protection against Russian domination. Nor could America default on the resultant obligations or retire into itself. Its interests in security and in maintaining its own relative prosperity forced it to concern with world conditions. Moreover, its commitments prohibited nonchalant insensitiveness to the fate of others: interests, ethics, and concern for public reputation all drove us in the same direction. An earlier isolationism, such as was once reflected in our refusal of membership in the old League of Nations, proved impossible. The American heartland might be temporarily impregnable. But the two-ocean power was centrally located in a world of subcontinental states or confederations. It was in strategy and interest no longer at once removed from and attached to Europe alone. The latter, now in decline, was indeed far from irrelevant or impotent to distract. We ourselves could no longer turn our back on Europe in order to purify and utilize the talents of its inheritance against the backdrop of an unbounded horizon. But we could also not look in one direction alone.

While war was still being waged, we were the leading architects of the United Nations. Likewise, Americans largely devised the economic bases of a postwar international policy which was intended to support and sustain that new way of international life. The financial-economic design of Bretton Woods, the preliminary drafting of Dumbarton Oaks, and the final conference at San Francisco constituted a pattern for international action with American sponsorship and support. Whatever the practical reasons for choice of those places, their locations symbolize the range and directions of our new outlook as world power.

More importantly, American membership and participation in the United Nations seemed to indicate an abandonment of isolationism and an acceptance of the concept of the nation's international interest. Similarly, the fact that our delegates were variously former ambassadors, politicians, career bureaucrats, or distinguished private citizens drafted for the job gave notice of our recognition of the essentially social and co-organic nature of the American nation. Moreover, in view of America's position of leadership, the design for international loans for the development of undeveloped countries and the inclusion in the United Nations Charter itself of provisions for international action and co-operation in economic and social affairs alike seemed to reflect a changed attitude, even though the economic powers granted the new organization were deliberately limited. The novel arrangements suggested a clear awareness on our part of the interdependence of peoples.

They indicated our manifest intent to pursue coherent and rational economic policies. They gave further endorsement to the idea of co-partnership between government and private enterprise, with government as the regulating partner. Certainly the contrast with the old League and the abandonment of Wilson's moralistic and doctrinaire international individualism were clear enough. Indeed, subsequent ideological conflict with the U.S.S.R. and its own deep-rooted suspicion of our motives arose largely from these specific courses. Our own cosponsorship of the veto was given in part on grounds of security for the antitotalitarian and individualistic co-partnership view of the state, even though in the event it proved unfortunate. It doubtless furthered Russian distrust of our motives, even as the veto itself provided a valuable weapon in the Communist armory. Our subsequent views of the nature and content of an international bill of rights completed the process of political and philosophical alienation. For, from the Russian viewpoint, which here constitutes signal testimony to our intent and accomplishment, the United Nations was an organization manifestly designed by the West to promote through co-operative governmental action the preservation of a modified system of private enterprise on individualist assumptions. The institutional provisions for international financing and promotion of economic welfare left no room for doubt: they were on Communist premises a subtly sinister, because seemingly statesmanlike and enlightened, imposition of capitalism in the name of international peace and order.

Subsequent direct American aid in the relief, reconstruction, and finally rearmament of Europe was a necessary consequence of America's position, of the urgency of time, and of the awkward slowness of new institutions. It was also a commentary on the partial irrelevance of those institutions in a situation where the United States alone could provide the needed goods and foot the bills. Our new undertakings rested on a broad concept of international interdependence and of America's international interest. They involved also our acceptance of the primacy of political judgment and governmental action, of a close relating of internal and external affairs, and of the need for a coherent directing by indirection of the course of private enterprise. They were conceived for the promotion of a national interest based on concepts of interdependence between our home political economy and the economic welfare and political stability of members of our own bloc. They were dedicated to the securing at once of morale and of effective power throughout the membership of that bloc. They were directed to bolstering our own national security and to the protection and promotion of our internal business economy. That economy actually prospered under the resultant burdens.

Our commitments, then, were based on a theory of international interest. Our power and our contribution to the collective good were preponderant. But our doctrine of leadership was grounded in deliberate commitment to United Nations as the normal vehicle for collective action. It made us simply the senior ally. Our rapid return to a decontrolled system of individualistic normalcy after World War II would probably have necessitated reimposition of controls at home in any emergency. But the very range and indefiniteness of our commitments made the speedy devising and imposition of such controls imperative. We had to avoid runaway inflation. For our own and the overall good we had to utilize with maximum efficiency our resources and productive capacity which, though vast, were not inexhaustible and could not be expanded with sufficient rapidity to make ourselves and our allies immediately secure against hostile threats. Our commitments tended to outrun our immediately available productive capacities. That situation gave aid and comfort both to isolationists and to individualists who desired to measure such commitments by narrowly economic criteria. Always inimical to controls, the individualist had an especially strong case when controls meant obvious sacrifices and yet were obviously inadequate to solve positively the total problem of world economic rehabilitation and development.

Nevertheless, on grounds of security and stabilization, such controls were once more accepted with good grace as immediately necessary, even though they were modified at the demand of various interests, and in the name of maximum freedom and flexibility for enterprise under the unsought but imposed conditions. Yet fears of peacetime statism, criticisms of extravagance and corruption, doctrines of sound finance, and a desire for defined commitments proved strong. Under the aegis of party strife exacerbated by the Republican party's long years in the wilderness, they combined with surviving isolationist feeling to produce an emphatic revival of individualistic and free-enterprise sentiment. They led to forceful attacks on the newer reinterpretation of national interest as international. And in due course they led to the removal, or radical modification, of the controls.

Fears of statism and of a purely governmental interpretation of the national interest were part of the motivation underlying such criticism and policy change, as was also moral concern over corruption and waste. But the basic indictment rested on individualistic preconceptions. It involved a failure to accept the concept of co-partnership either in domestic or in foreign affairs. The balanced budget and the absence of a significant national debt had, indeed, alike become improbable. Nevertheless the relevant stereotypes continued to have force as myth or pretended and delusive aspiration. They variously inspired sensible demands for efficiency in military spending; the search for purely American preparedness and self-defense; and criticism of the volume, the conditions, and the purposes of aid to allies, whether for their internal reconstruction or for rearmament.

Hopes for a return to a purely individualistic system of international economic relations had indeed been abandoned. No one proposed that banks and investment houses should take over the job of negotiating loans to foreign governments. Nor was it seriously suggested that financial institutions should decide in the light of their private economic judgments what enterprises in what countries should receive financing, and on what terms. For the lesson of the twenties had been learned. Moreover, for the most part the changed nature of foreign political economies, with their own developed governmental controls, precluded such activities. Still more importantly, however, this type of individualistic thinking had withered away almost unobserved. It had been replaced by a recognition that government was the organ and vehicle for the compounding and effectuation of the nation's external interests through economic, not less than through political and military, instrumentalities.

The individualistic viewpoint nevertheless reasserted itself in other ways. First, there arose a growing insistence that our own government should shape its assistance policies according to sound business judgments. It must treat its allies as parties to business contracts or as suitors for bank loans. Allies in turn were judged on their credit condition. That judgment, moreover, rested on their past or present practice as debtors. It was not based on their potential economic development or reconstruction, nor yet on their political stability and probable military value. Significantly, legislation was enacted to insure the narrower judgment. Great Britain was thereby driven to emulate the earlier practices which had brought unwarranted, or at least excessive, eulogies to Finland. The gains to Britain's own economy and the increase of its value as our ally were alike dubious.

The demand for such narrow and inappropriate policies rested in no small part on a prayerful hope to limit American commitments. It was also related to the desire to restrict the export of American products where it was suspected that they were being given away, with pointless loss in home consumption and in the American standards of living. Political isolationism was altogether impossible; but the use of the criteria of sound business in the conduct of its foreign policy at minimum economic cost was not. Proper concentration on the needs of consumers at home would insulate and preserve America's differential standards of living. Yet under the conditions of bipolar conflict, and given the aspirations and needs of other peoples, such a policy tended in the long run towards our self-imposed political isolation. It could at best be justified on the score that a strong internal economy would most effectively secure American power. That position had some warrant insofar as it meant ability to avoid an inflation which seemed otherwise inevitable and not to be controlled. But under the circumstances it was quite unwarranted insofar as it was designed to lead to further increases in consumption of goods and services. A people who, even under a different policy, would enjoy differentially high standards of living could not afford to alienate impoverished friends by conspicuous consumption.

No doubt the policy of hard-headedness received some support from very primitive mercantilist economic doctrine. The simple convictions that the wealth and power of a nation was enhanced by keeping gold at home and that to export money was to lose were by no means dead, even though we were all aware that our gold was buried in Fort Knox and that our loans would consist in capital goods and technical aid. Nevertheless, the idea of gaining and losing trades survived, whilst a conception of political economy relevant to our position in the new world order was still lacking. Indeed, our conscious doctrine was not concerned with the national role or our collective welfare. It rested solely on classical analysis: both parties should gain, and gain equally, from an exchange. Such mutual gain was to be assessed purely in monetary terms. The concept that benefits might arise from mutual political and collective power was either not envisioned or was specifically rejected. Rejection was facilitated by past experience. European governments and peoples had often shown lack of gratitude for American aid and generosity. Sometimes, indeed, they had been manifestly resentful that, by reason of greater resources and lesser involvement and war burdens, America was able to give such aid at all. Positively, the Samuel Smiles doctrine of self-help was applied to nations. But judgment as to whether those who received aid were actually using it adequately to help themselves rested on American standards of tempo and energies, which were utterly unrealistic when applied to most other peoples.

The relation of individualism and legalism

Behind these attitudes was a broader heritage, at once moralistic and legalistic. In origin it was European, but in intensity and rigidity it was peculiarly American. Its public side rested on the ancient doctrine, *pacta sunt servanda*. That doctrine was restated to mean that international agreements, whether formally treaties or not, ought to be kept, and kept *au pied de la lettre*. For Americans, it was given the status of dogma by reason of our individualistic legal and constitutional concept of the sanctity of contracts. The latter teaching had been appropriate to a society of nations, not less than to an internal economy, where the range and techniques of communication and economic exchange were still somewhat stable. But it continued to be applied with increasing inappropriateness to a world of ever-increasing tempo. To insure stabilized economies and stable régimes necessitated adapting international pacts and agreements in the light of changed conditions. Rigidity became the enemy of accommodating and creative statesmanship, not the expression of high principle.

Manifestly, neither treaties nor contracts should be broken on the whim of one party alone, or by reason of its greater power. That principle is fundamental to practical morality. It is a necessary basis for mutual confidence between peoples and persons. But the doctrine of the sanctity of treaties and contracts has also embraced as a minor premise an idea of permanence which is actually inimical to any true idea of justice in any order where change is of the essence. The premise was reasonably relevant in an age when legal individuals were persons, when life expectancy was briefer than today, and when the dominant social-economic order was agrarian. Nevertheless, Plato had long since shown, at the opening of *The Republic,* that even for the individual circumstances might be so changed as to render inadequate a definition of justice as the returning to a man of his own. That simple idea of Simonides which Socrates combatted was nevertheless on balance relevant, *mutatis mutandis,* to international relations at the time of the emergence and development of the European state system. For it provided a basis for the stability of a simple economy. It constituted rough justice under conditions where the rank and file of mankind were on the whole little affected by the doings and disturbances of princes. But in this age of applied science, general involvement in politics and conspicuous change of the scale and tempo of public life, the doctrine has become irrelevant and burdensome. Its inadequacy is demonstrated by the impossible position of small states in the present-day world, where they survive by the tolerance or through the balancings of their great neighbors. It is revealed by the great difficulties of effective maintenance of the European nation-states system in general.

The static rigidity of sacrosanct treaties and contracts does not today insure that predictability which is the social rationale of such sanctity. Rather, in the name of security and honor, such a rigid system endeavors to preserve an individualistic ideology now divorced from its proper corollary and complement, creative and socially rewarding risk-taking. Its actual consequence is to assure insecurity through inevitable shocks consequent on unadaptability. The inescapability of changed conditions, relations, and needs renders its attempted permanent vesting of interests and its defense of once-established status as dishonorable as it is inexpedient.

While treaties are in our time often denounced and terminated, there has been a major failure to provide workable techniques for revisions and readjustments in most of the basic agreements between nations. This failure is due in part to inadequacies in institutional machinery. It is due even more to inadequate understanding of the actual relationships between states and to inappropriate concepts for the conduct of international relations. Today the United States has a real obligation, as it has the opportunity, to take a lead in overcoming these deficiencies in order to further effectively its own international interest. Yet its doctrine of the sanctity of agreements stands in the way. That doctrine is buttressed by a literalism and legalistic rigidity which stems from the needs of business faith and from a misapplication of ideas of risk-taking and bankruptcy.

Disputes over what constitutes good faith in relation to currency and credit have, indeed, run like a clear thread through American history. At least one segment of our society has, from Colonial days, seen the inadequacy and injustice under changing conditions of a rigid, "sound" currency. But the implications for all business arrangements have still not been fully drawn. Far less have they been generally accepted. Indeed, despite considerable contemporary indignation, John Marshall's extreme insistence on the sanctity and unchangeability of contracts has received and continues to receive a widespread and largely unconscious acceptance as it is applied to business affairs. Today it has also become part of the more general individualistic and legalistic climate of opinion within which we function both in domestic and in international affairs. It has buttressed our conviction of the sanctity of treaties and international obligations and has, in some sort, become identified with it.

Nevertheless, men have in their private economic affairs refused to accept such dogma as binding, where the consequence was widespread ruin. Their unwillingness was clearly revealed, for instance, during the great depression, when Midwestern farmers frustrated attempted foreclosures. Yet, for all the pragmatism and sociological realism which informs modern American legal thought, men's actual behaviors and the practical folly of pushing dogma to disastrous conclusions have brought no change in our myth or in the political-economic stereotypes by which we so largely conduct our affairs. Indeed, while much of the current criticism of public borrowing and expenditure no doubt rests on proper fears of inflation, the resentment at a fifty-cent dollar is to a considerable degree based on a feeling that money ought not, whatever the circumstances, to change its value. Men are entitled to receive what they contracted for. But because of symbol thinking, the logical inference that it is necessary to revise contracts when inescapable changes in conditions prevent a constant currency is not drawn. Irving Fisher's old proposal of a wholesale price change index as a basis for long-term contracts has never been accepted. The refusal is partly due to the seeming threat to the dogma of contractual sanctity.

Our legal thinking remains, in short, dominantly individualistic and static. Yet the results of its application to a society of corporate groups and to a world of nations which, in the main, do not die, but whose relations and circumstances constantly change, make clear the need for a new public law divorced from individualistic legalisms. In certain areas of domestic policy, we are already approaching a different viewpoint, as voluntary reopening by employers of labor contracts, where no clause necessitates such action, readily reveals. Commission regulation, as well as much of the general procedure of administrative law, indicates similar trends. All of these adaptive procedures, it may be noted, take place under concepts of a social interest as the true national interest. They properly involve a rejection of statism as the state personified and individualized. They involve likewise a rejection of absolute individualism, which makes the legal person a microcosmic state. Similarly, they escape that curious position which characterized early constitutionalism on individualist premises, whereby the state became itself a warrant for individual imperialism through its guaranteeing of near-absolute rights.

Unfortunately, in the realm of American international relations the ancient dogmas continue to inspire politics. They constitute limits on policy and hindrances to the effective implementation of newer insights by those whose experience reveals the evils of intransigent rigidity. In that area, what Thurman Arnold properly called the "folklore of capitalism" continues to enjoy an anachronistic heyday.

There legalism is indeed buttressed by the whole American constitutional system. It has often been remarked that, once questions of social policy reach the level of possible public action through law, they tend to be debated on the grounds of probable finding of consonance or otherwise with the Constitution, rather than of ethics or of expediency. While that difficulty still besets us in the conduct of our internal affairs, where we alone are the parties involved, we have discovered means to circumvent the embarrassments arising from our formal devotion. To that end we have used the politics of legislation, amply endowed with legal talent; the politics of judicial appointment; and the politics of the highest level of the judiciary, the Supreme Court, which may not indeed follow but does not utterly neglect the election returns. But in our dealings with foreign affairs, a like accommodation has not occurred. There we are inexperienced in leadership, and analogous institutions and political practices remain at best in embryo. Consequently our constitutionalist legalism in dealing with public issues buttresses our legalism in construing private commitments and rights. It thereby gets in the way of an expediential morality of adjustment and concession serviceable to our international interest and creative of good will and understanding.

Hitherto we have not learned the fundamental lesson which Edmund Burke endeavored to teach England in the hope that the American Colonies might be kept within the empire, namely, that legal rights are often political and moral wrongs. For they do disservice to real interests. Hence legalistic concepts become the enemies of statesmanship, where they should be its supports. Great Britain learned the lesson. She was no doubt aided by the absence of a written constitution, since in the realm of external relations such a constitution facilitates rigidity. In its imperial policies England has moved from a legalism which disrupts to a mysticism which preserves. In the conduct of foreign relations that country has avoided the inconveniences of unadaptive principle. As a consequence, it has suffered bad reputation but has achieved good results. We have yet to learn the obvious lesson. Our lasting success as leader of the West and of the world depends on our learning it rapidly. For it is fundamental to the effective development of coherence between our internal and our international policies. It is vital to a sound and effective defense of this nation's interest as a democratic political society, determined to avoid the statist way.

IV

Hindrances to policy: Nationalistic self-interest and power politics

 ───────────────────────────────

The two historic hindrances to an effective American foreign policy, isolationism and individualism, were dissimilar both in ethos and in genesis. Today they paradoxically tend to make common cause as subordinate supports for a viewpoint inherited from Europe, and fundamentally inimical alike to our tradition and to our moral purpose in the world.

Individualism, which is so deep and lasting an element in our thought patterns and in the practice of our society, is basically, and almost by definition, antistatist. It was begotten and brought to these shores as a protest against that corruption of the Reformation which made the ruler of the state the selector and head of its established and monopolizing religion. It was given further breeding and broadening here as protest against religious dogma imposed as social discipline and enforced by the public authority of a self-appointed and co-opting aristocracy which deemed itself elect. It developed as a secular political philosophy of protest against executive arbitrariness, and then against all distant and uncomprehending government, executive or legislative. It became in due course a plea for free venturing and creative use of energies in the social-economic realm, whereby men might improve their lot through the opportunities offered by an open frontier and untouched resources. Finally, and most generally, it was transformed into their right to freedom of movement and action throughout the world, unrestrained by their own or by other governments. The view that it was the sufficient obligation of our government as maker of foreign policy to protect and further that claim in due course constituted a hindrance to American effectiveness as a moral leader in the world. It became a threat to our own economic well-being at home, and a source of insecurity in our international relations, economic and political.

Individualism, isolationism, and national interest

Individualism as freedom to venture abroad is today no adequate basis for foreign policy. For effective pursuit of our purposes necessitates coherent and positive action by government as protector and promoter of the interests of the nation as a broadly social, rather than a narrowly political, order. Nevertheless, some modern individualists have become friends of a foreign policy which is at once nationalistic and isolationist. They are aware that, quite apart from any interventions with their enterprise abroad by the American government, the attitudes and policies of other governments do not permit them a free hand or free trade, nor give them any assurance of subsequent noninterference even when they have been permitted to venture. Their defense of individualism as a basis for foreign policy has become largely negative, an attempt to prevent governmental use of national resources for international purposes. That stand is essentially a part of their more fundamental purpose, to protect or restore a system of pure free enterprise at home. For they are convinced that the social welfare state necessarily leads to centralization of power in the hands of the federal government, to state socialism, and at last to total statism. They are completely unaware that, as public welfare government, it may constitute the one available road to the avoidance of statism after the European pattern. Hence they attack its bureaucracy, its social welfare program, and its taxation in the name of freedom of enterprise and of effective opportunities for private capital accumulation and investment. By a like token, they indict its foreign policy, and in particular its participation as leader and chief financial backer of reconstruction in Europe and of assistance in the development of backward countries. They view such undertakings, in large measure correctly, as an extension of the social welfare philosophy. They see that extension as a further burden on the taxpayer, a further draining of funds otherwise available for enterprise, a further strengthening of the stranglehold of government over society, and a most sinister exploitation of idealism in the service of statism. Such undertakings are peculiarly bad since the beneficiaries are foreigners, not their fellow citizens. The latter, in a futile effort to help others to economic well-being as a basis for freedom, themselves become enslaved. In the name of individualism at home, therefore, the critics urge the need for withdrawal of public aid to peoples abroad. In this respect they support isolationism. They proclaim an exclusive national interest, to be secured by the power and wealth of an internal economy freed from government, and for enterprise.

Such individualist isolationists are necessarily aware of bipolar tension. Indeed, more than others they are frantically fearful of Russian aggression against this nation and of attack on its cities and industries. They therefore urge the need for a strong defense to repel and defeat aggression by air and to deliver counterblows in the same medium. They question whether a Europe unwilling or unable on its own to defend itself from Russian attack by land would be any more willing to do so by reason of our subsidizing its forces. Given such unwillingness, the increased ability we had provided would either be lost to us or would become a source of strength against us. They are, moreover, convinced that to send over American ground forces to fight a Russian invader of Western Europe would be absurd. Even were the logistics problem capable of solution, the requisite forces would either arrive too late or would in the best of cases suffer quite disproportionate losses. Whether there would be any long-term gains from their ultimate triumph is in any case doubtful. Meanwhile, the nation would be continuously under arms. Young men's normal lives and careers would have to be interrupted for an indefinite period to come. Our economy could not be freed from government interventions. The tax burden would be overwhelming and beyond reduction. A large air force, capable of defense and counterattack, is the cheapest insurance of American security. It also involves minimum interference at once with individual lives and with the individualist economy.

As noted earlier, many supporters of this individualist and isolationist doctrine have taken a position in relation to the Far East which is seemingly inconsistent with their philosophy. Yet the inconsistency is more apparent than real. In Western Europe most established governments appear potentially capable of resistance against possible Russian aggression if they had the will. But their peoples give evidence of some uncertainty in allegiance to their present institutions. In any event, the régimes seem destined to tend towards socialism and the abandonment of the individualistic way. Moreover, in Europe our thorough participation in an all-out land war is by precedent a possible adventure. In Asia, on the other hand, and specifically in China, the situation is far different. Communism, the most extreme form of statism, and our avowed enemy, has established itself in China by Russian-aided revolution against a *de jure* government. The nationalist government of Chiang Kai-Shek, in exile but established in Formosa, has a will to counterrevolution but little other interest or hope. Despite America's leading part in the Korean war, whose initiation and conduct most of the isolationist group deplored, there is little realistic possibility of our total involvement in an all-out land war in China and Eastern Russia, as there are no precedents. Hence aid to Chiang is support of one who, if not a committed supporter of individualism, is at least a convinced opponent of its arch-enemy. It can be given without any real prospect of our own general military involvement, and it is directed against an advancing enemy. The costs are limited. The policy complements the idea of isolation and air defense. Indeed Chiang is in that area the loose equivalent of such defense.

Nevertheless, such an attitude towards American concerns in the Far East is not a policy of pure isolationism at the present time. It is, however, consistent with ultimate American withdrawal from all foreign commitments. It buttresses the search for an American way of life which is for ourselves alone and not for export. Such a life is to be lived while necessary under the protective umbrella of a vast and specialized defensive air force, whose shadow is security. The theme, in any event, is the vital importance of restoring and preserving an individualist capitalism at home. To that end it is necessary to diminish the actual scope of activities by the federal government. This purpose can be partially accomplished by removing a major justification for its broad functioning and imposed controls through abandonment of those foreign policies which render such activities clearly necessary.

The securing of individualism requires, then, an ideal of isolation, a present policy of using buffers where possible and profitable to insulate ourselves by limited commitments of resources and withdrawal or refusal of armed aid, and by an abandonment of the right of private venturing abroad. Nevertheless some of the supporters of this type of policy regard it, not as the path to Shangri-La isolationism, but as a temporary measure to live out the storm. They hope and believe that a manifest unconcern with the world's problems on the part of America will rob the U.S.S.R. of its fears of American aggression, and will in any event diminish the force of its propaganda against us elsewhere, as would-be imperialists. Their theory is that a narrow self-interest on our part will not promote an aggressive alliance by the rest of the world against us, motivated by envy. Rather, it will decrease tensions. It will strengthen the free world by not forcing uncommitted peoples to choose between becoming either satellites to Russia or unequal partners with ourselves, both of which are resented. Soviet Communism, with no positive rival, will find its ideological imperialism impotent. For no country or people would seek its dubious blessings and endure the shocking transformation of their established culture if they confronted as an alternative the neutral enjoyment of their accustomed ways. Once the crisis is past, and the U.S.S.R. is deprived of the opportunity to avoid or ignore internal discontents by the plausible claim of insecurity for its system through the expansion of our own, it will be possible for us to return to our tradition of freedom for our business interests to venture at will in the world. In the long run we shall have avoided both statism at home and a system of international economic, as well as political, relations under government control and direction. The trend of such internationalism is likewise in the long run statist. Indeed, it may well lead towards a world state, with grim consequences alike for the American and for other peoples.

Whether the ultimate objective is isolation with internal free enterprise or whether it is a world made safe for individualism thanks to our minding our own business, the proponents of the immediate policies above described seem to be in agreement that it is improper for the United States to promote social welfare enterprises and governments throughout the free world and at American expense. Even the realization that national security may depend on positive international security does not warrant such a course. Nevertheless, these critics recognize that for some time to come individual venturings abroad must be curtailed or abandoned. They grant the concession the more readily since the attitudes of other governments make such venturings generally impractical on the normal calculations of business risk. They insist, however, that statist economies abroad are buttressed or encouraged by our own present policies. For the moment, in any event, a temporary and partial self-denying ordinance by our business world is a necessary price of a lasting restoration of individualism. Finally, they are agreed that it is proper for our own government to make loans to other governments for specific purposes according to their credit, and for us to assume the role of a prudent investment banker, wherever other powers show promise of self-protection, of service to the individualist and American interest in resistance to Russia, and of good business faith. Such public enterprise is necessary by reason of the present condition of the world. It is not social welfare statism, since it strictly follows the motivations of individualism. Only in technique is it a departure from the long-lived practice of government guaranteed loans, which are part of the modern individualist pattern. In its pure forms, this whole viewpoint is clearly recessive today. Its lack of broad appeal was most obviously revealed at the 1952 party conventions in the planks of both parties and by the selection of candidates committed to more positive and participating foreign policies. The outcome of those decisions is not necessarily a bipartisan foreign policy. Indeed, such political behavior is unlikely, as it is undesirable, if by bipartisanship is meant absence of criticism and of dissent on specific actions. But bipartisanship in the Vandenberg sense, more properly to be designated non-partisanship, is to a large degree a present fact. Its reality does not, however, betoken a refusal to the isolationist minority of the right of criticism and dissent. For to Vandenberg, bipartisan policy meant that government should provide the opposition with information necessary to enlightened and informed discussion of real issues. It meant consultation between leaders of both parties and with State Department officials in order to prevent false or merely partisan conflicts. It meant an attempt to achieve a united national stand where American interests created a common cause which transcended party differences. It meant the deliberate acceptance of an underlying consensus as to our leadership and responsibility in the world.

Today individualistic isolationism is increasingly impotent by itself alone. But it is also a special formulation, plausibly rooted in American tradition, of a broader and different attitude towards international relations which derives from the European nation-state system. That attitude has been re-stated to fit the superficial facts and the surface patterns of American political life. This broader concept goes under the name of national interest. It is ultimately inconsistent with American individualism, as respect for personality, and with our long-lived social pluralism. For it grounds national interest in the claimed reality of power politics, as that phrase is commonly understood. The resultant philosophy, which also has many adherents in the anti-isolationist camp, appeals to an American prejudice in favor of hard-headed realism and of practicality. It combats an equal prejudice in favor of moral idealism by making policies oriented towards international co-operation and American responsibility for Western leadership and the welfare of free régimes elsewhere appear impractical, starry-eyed idealism. It denounces such policies as pointless and thankless abandonment of the interests of the United States, without proportionate recompense. In the extreme, it accuses their proponents of disloyalty and lack of patriotism, and insists that they are persons who put another interest above our own.

The position gains plausibility and elicits an almost unthinking consent on a review of the pattern of liberal thought prevalent above all in these United States, but to a considerable extent also in England and Western Europe, from the Wilson period down to the invasion of Poland, or even till Pearl Harbor. It is further buttressed by an examination of actual policies and actions in international affairs by ourselves, as also, again to a lesser extent, by some of our present allies. The beginning of such attitudes and policies may conveniently be dated from America's entry into the First World War, with the avowed objective of making the world safe for democracy. That undertaking, far nobler in motive than a later and celebrated moralistic experiment, ended in disillusion consequent on the postwar revelation of the motives and secret agreements of our allies; and on their subsequent narrowly self-interested conduct. Indeed, it appeared almost irrelevant as a consequence of the actual failure of democracy to spread, and its seeming propensity to contract its area of effective operations. The conviction became widespread that we had in fact been dupes. We were grievously misled by what was at best a naïve idealism and at worst an unwarranted self-righteousness which drove us, for all our inexperience in European affairs, to play the meddling and muddling busybody. Wilson himself had been too assured of his own integrity and the rightness of his purpose. He had proved incapable of calling the bluff or firmly resisting the pressure of his Big Four colleagues. He had surrendered a genuine chance to attain America's professed war aim by making concessions to immoral realism in order to secure a document which he believed would create a living corrective institution.

America did indeed fail to bring into being a better and more stable world based on moral principle and its own lasting vision. Nevertheless, it is conceivable that that failure was not the result of a naïve idealism and lack of concern for our own national interest in a world of national rivalries and hates. It may well have been caused by a needless surrender to realism and a lack of sure commitment to principled integrity. Conceivably our failure to join the League of Nations prevented the recovery of lost ground in the way Wilson had hoped. But on such an interpretation our abstention becomes in the event a proper unwillingness to endorse Europe's realistic statesmanship, even though the motivation for refusing to join was an equally narrow realism and a more negativistic emulation of European policies.

The excesses of liberal internationalism

Nevertheless, the fact of the League, acceptance of the Wilson thesis, resentment at the little band of stubborn men, and the actualities of American power and American interests in Europe combined to preserve and to foster liberal idealism in international relations. So, too, did the actual exposure of the realities of European politics. The recognition of those realities, especially when combined with effective muckraking of the so-called merchants of death, begot moral resentment and a determination to secure reform. We evinced a determination to be different by abandoning utterly the instrumentalities which had led to such abuses. Early in the postwar period, Americans sincerely espoused the erroneous belief that a good example was as effective a technique of moral training in the world of states as it was in the family circle. That belief led to the noble folly of disarmament, partially achieved as an outcome of the Washington Naval Conference. The results of such action did indeed convey an effective warning of the dangers of misguided idealism. They gave strong support to the defenders of national interest and opponents of idealism. Yet whether in the long run our desire to set a peaceful example without recompense harmed this country more than the competitive search for power of the earlier "We Want Eight" campaign harmed England is surely open to question. The latter indulgence in competitive naval armament surely heightened Anglo-German rivalry, and helped create an atmosphere which facilitated the coming of the First World War. In any event, our own error was one in means and technique rather than in objective.

The subsequent Kellogg Pact, for all its nobility of aspiration, revealed an equally misguided faith in the efficacy of resounding declarations. For a moment it deluded many persons into the belief that lasting peace had been attained. Thereby it hampered rather than helped the practical and realistic work of statesmen in diminishing specific tensions and in coping with actual conflicts of interest. More generally, indeed, the liberal idealists of the inter-war years talked and behaved as though public resolutions, and formal American adherence to international institutions such as the League and the World Court, would in themselves assure peace. What is more, they often took the position that honest signature or adherence and a demonstration that the United States was unaggressive by rendering it impotent for defense, yet alone attack, would eliminate envy of its wealth. Rather, such actions would create a nobler envy of its moral ascendency. Thereby they would persuade other nations to abandon their mutual suspicions, their traditional rivalries, and their respective drives to expansion.

In the universities, a number of student generations were taught international relations as moral principles of world peace, the potential splendors of the League, the wickedness of departure from Wilsonian doctrines, the evils of imperialism and dollar diplomacy, and the efficacy of popular demands for a better world and for a change of heart. Not infrequently, too, they learned the rightness of pacifism, the power of nonviolence, the uselessness of force, and the sinfulness of power politics, though in this country these teachings did not culminate in their quite logical outcome, the Oxford Oath. Nevertheless, one of their consequences was widespread contempt for military men and a resentment at programs of military training. Any talk of preparedness was militarism, and so constituted a threat to the peace of the world and to freedom at home. Happily, when the need arose, these impressions proved powerless against experience, practical necessity, and national pride and allegiance. Moreover, moral hatred of aggressors, which was also among the lessons learned, actually gave support to war against Germany and Japan. Nevertheless, recognition by our people of the threat of Hitlerism to ourselves came slowly. It was a hard achievement of persuasion and experience. Clearly, the views prevalent in the thirties resulted in an initial unpreparedness on our part. When the crisis broke that unpreparedness was rapidly offset by reason of effective industrial organization, superior technology, a well-trained labor force, and greater resources. Yet needless sacrifices and losses were suffered in the interim.

Moreover, doctrines that good will and decency generally prevailed in the world, and only needed strengthening, created suspicion of any attempt to organize our power for defense and for effective influence on others. They likewise resulted in unbelief in ambitions and philosophies alien to our ways, and in the reality of evil. As a consequence, we showed a pathetic willingness to take at face value expedient professions of good will or like-mindedness, even when their authors were manifestly unbenevolent dictators. Here again, we did not stand alone. But the sins of lack of conservative and lack of liberal imagination undoubtedly prevented realism in our dealings first with Hitler's Germany, and then with Stalin's Russia. Indeed, the seeds of the last error were sown even before Hitler loomed on our horizon and assaulted our consciences. Our desire for peace and good will led us to deny that political philosophies and programs based on hate and directed to inculcating hate could be meant literally or intended as bases for action. We professed frank unbelief that Hitler meant what he said in *Mein Kampf*. For long we ignored the real horrors perpetrated by dictators, while we laughed at their public posturings. We also refused for a considerable period to take seriously our own colored shirt movements, or anti-American fifth-column conspiracies. Many Americans accepted periodic Communist professions of shared purpose and common faith as sincere. They took as proof of their genuineness any and every expedient and temporary acceptance of our rules of the game.

In any event, the whole story, too well and sadly known to warrant detailed repetition, has through the successive shocks of Hitlerism and present-day Soviet Communism led to a serious discrediting of the earlier liberal dogmas. It has also brought many liberals of that time and place to a belated repentance. Unfortunately, that repentance has played into the hands of the advocates of a policy of furthering and protecting an exclusive national interest by means of pressure backed by force. They argue that the United Nations must necessarily follow the path of the League. Any genuine adherence to it, any support of it, any attempt to work through its institutions beyond the demands of expediency and convenience from the viewpoint of a purely American interest, lead to betrayal of this country's real interests. Such policies sacrifice our own well-being in the service of internationalism, which, their opponents maintain, is still today as naïve and futile an aspiration as it proved formerly. In support of that contention, they instance the horrible wranglings in United Nations meetings, which provide an international sounding board for Soviet propaganda, and the extraordinary difficulties confronted in circumventing the Soviet use of the veto. The more extreme among them urge that without the incubus of the United Nations we could readily have protected our interests and made expedient agreements with other powers, who for the moment had parallel interests. We could have avoided needless delays and wastes of energy which resulted from public international debate. We could have avoided lasting commitments which tie our hands and hamper our actions. Such critics conveniently forget that we ourselves supported, and indeed cosponsored, the veto in the name of protection of national interest against a possible ganging up against us by other powers.

Liberal internationalists of the inter-war years tended also to be friends of the Soviet Union. They looked on its revolution as a hopeful search for greater justice and equality in the world. At the very least they felt it was actually producing a marvellous advance towards the betterment of the Russian peoples in comparison with their condition under the reactionary Czarist régime. Consequently, they hopefully advocated diplomatic recognition, which was in due course achieved. They worked continuously for greater co-operation between the two nations, for more trade and for greater cultural interchange. They consistently urged tolerance of the Communist party in the United States, on the ground that Russia also enjoyed, or would progressively achieve, a free constitutional government. This whole attitude, now largely abandoned, gives further aid and comfort to the current proponents of policies based on exclusive national interest. In particular, it makes opposition or criticism by repentant liberals difficult, especially since a small minority have failed to repent, despite every warrant for disillusionment. For the past error is now manifest; as is the error of those who, whatever their initial justification or excusable succumbing to deception, belatedly continue to insist that Communism in China is an agrarian movement in ethos closer to the British Levellers and Diggers of the seventeenth century than to the Communist party line.

The proponents of national interest argue, and the repentant fear, that past errors may be repeated. Aspiration to the achievement of a better world by means of policies based on good will appears folly. It is futile to regard international organization as anything more than an extension of conventional techniques of diplomacy or a convenient locus for their exercise. For the peaceful and collaborative professions of others are never to be trusted, and cannot be demonstrated. They are temporarily useful weapons in the service of purely selfish national interests and ambitions. For the United States to profess and pursue a wider and nobler goal than others are prepared to seek and further is voluntarily to burden itself with a debilitating source of relative weakness. Indeed, our best course, and our greatest contribution to human welfare, is to emulate the rest of the world and to look to our own interests. Our sole responsibilities are to husband and increase America's wealth; to protect and cherish its freedom; and to develop and enjoy its own peculiar culture.

The sins of liberal internationalists prior to World War II are in retrospect clear enough. In the name of idealism, such seekers for a

better world were in truth utopian. They did not indeed deny evils in
the past practice of governments and interest groups. Rather, they
tended to overemphasize the sinister motives of those then in power.
Nevertheless, in dealing with immediate international problems, they
were all too ready to take professions of good intent for accomplishment, or for guarantees of future accomplishment and proofs of
change of heart. Proclaimed or intended goodness on the part of other
governments rendered force unnecessary, and so warranted our own
abandonment of the means to apply it. Liberal utopianism thus became
a theory and practice for the present. It was not simply a matter of
belief in the possibility that a perfected world society could be attained
at some future date. The internationalists queerly combined together
the incantations of Coué and a distorted vulgarization of the "as if"
philosophy of Hans Vaihinger: they preached, and where able prac-
ticed, the view that to behave as if men and nations were ideally good
and sinless would rapidly make that vain assumption actual fact.

They were no doubt right to take the position that force is in the
spiritual realm irrelevant and incompetent, as in the moral realm it is
ultimately evil. In this sense they were morally superior and analytically
correct as against those who proclaimed that force was good in itself;
or asserted, more modestly, yet even more dangerously, that it was indifferent. Force may be used to succor the practice and the practitioners of morality. But its necessity is evidence of evil in the world. Its
employment, however necessary, is an inescapable limitation on the
attainment of perfect good and a sure evidence of its absence. That
realization, indeed, was one of the great insights of Christian teaching
in the political realm from St. Augustine on. It was at the root of the
medieval Two Powers doctrine, in its heyday so brilliantly devised to
prevent abuse of power through lack of humility. By very reason of
its nature and purpose, the Church could not use physical force. Yet
for his earthly ordering, finite and sinful man had to do so. The state
was always inferior, external, and instrumental because force was its
ultimate and proper means. Yet it was a necessary institution for man's
material and moral welfare. It was therefore justified in its works insofar as its force was employed in the service of moral good. It had

a duty to use force. Yet it was thereby inescapably contaminated and debarred from perfection, as men in earthly society were debarred from perfection. The liberal internationalists, correct in their search for world law and in their view as to the character of force, totally forgot or ignored this whole teaching. They were in error as to the possibilities of man's earthly accomplishment. They confused a rational end with practical achievement. They did not see that their ethic was, as Reinhold Niebuhr characterized Christian ethics, an impossible possibility.

That failure had disastrous consequences when translated into policy. It has by reaction given aid and comfort to the proponents of doctrines of exclusive national interest and power politics. It has done so not least by the defection to the realist camp of many liberal internationalists who are aware of the errors of the past and of a consequent skirting of disaster, but are yet not fully clear as to the nature of those errors. In essence, the ethical failure through misguided optimism was also a failure of historical insight. The search for an order of world law, founded on principle and sanctioned by force, was and is a reasonable quest. But human nature abhors a social vacuum: it is necessary to maintain and further existing constitutional régimes in order to avoid the rule of arbitrary power based on force alone. Only through principled power backed by force is it possible to create a better, a wider, and a more uniform world law. To abandon present imperfect institutions in the name of aspiration to a more far-reaching and morally better system is practically and morally erroneous. For the result is emptiness first; and then, through privation of available goods, the reign of evil.

Yet many internationalists argued that a prerequisite to world-wide law and order was abandonment by nations of concern for their particular interests. For such concern is inherently selfish, biased, and corrupt. It is therefore incompatible with justice. In plain truth, however, man is a creature of interests. His life is built on local attachments, particular experiences, and specific aspirations. The relativity of his position does limit his vision and his understanding. It is in an immediate sense the basis of what theologians call his proneness to sin.

But it is also the fulcrum of his action. By the use of reason he may indeed broaden his horizons, perceive and pursue a universal good, and attain some degree of disinterestedness. Yet he cannot utterly emancipate himself from the biases of place, time, and heritage. Moreover, should he reject his particular and local goods and attachments he achieves only a new bias, and in the process destroys his leverage for effective action towards a better condition of man. To maintain existing law and order and to have a decent respect for his own and his nation's interest is a precondition to extending the one and broadening the other. By such means alone may the particular interests of different peoples be reconciled, and the common good of humanity at large be increasingly achieved.

The doctrine that a dynamic but gradual harmonization of interests is the only path to international betterment is opposed both to utopianism and to a merely selfish pursuit of national interest through power politics. Indeed, advocates of the latter course gain appeal and command consent by reason of the manifest errors of a misguided utopianism which denies the value and the inescapability of national interest and rejects the utility and usability of generated power. A nation has interests, even though its people, a majority for the moment dominant, the statesmen who speak and act for it, or powerful interests within it may misinterpret what will in fact best serve those interests. Interpreters of the national interest may in the event prove wrong, even though their interpretations rested on an honest intent to serve it. Their judgment may be bad. Subsequent developments, genuinely unpredictable at the time, may cause policies which appeared serviceable to result in actual harm.

Normally, too, a nation will pursue its supposed or felt interests. Even the view that a nation ought not to be concerned with its peculiar interests is presumably conceived as being the real moral interest of its people, though such a teaching rests on inadequate ethics and does disserve to moral as well as practical interests. Though utopians may seek for what is in truth powerlessness in the name of pure moral principle unbacked by any sanction save its own appeal and consequent potency, politics is always and necessarily a matter of power. While conviction, habit, and interest can generate and husband power, its secure preservation rests ultimately on the availability of force, actual or potential. To talk of powerless politics would be a plain contradiction in terms. Hence, the concepts of national interest and power politics properly command an immediate consent as facts of public life. The combatting of teachings supposedly grounded in recognition of those facts and using those terms becomes peculiarly difficult, since opposition seems on its face to involve error and reveal idiocy.

The perversion of nationalism

Unfortunately, the contemporary defense of these concepts too frequently rests on a position as extreme as utopian internationalism or universalism. Likewise, it leads to courses of action at least as deleterious to the long-run interests of the nation, and even more harmful to humanity at large. It rests on a static view of history. It denies the relevance of moral aspiration. It insists that the relations of peoples are not informed, and cannot be informed, by morality as a sustained mutual interest. The nation-state is a permanent fact. Its nature does not change, though individual nations may change their interests, old nations may disappear, and new ones arise. Each nation developed separately; each remains separate; each has interests different from all others; each pursues, or ought to pursue, those interests regardless of others, or in opposition to them; each has, or can generate, a certain power whose basis is force; each has an obligation to generate and use that power to the maximum. Success in that venture is the only measure of right: each nation has an exclusive interest in its own well-being, and other nations are at best conveniences for the furtherance, or impediments to the attainment, of its interests.

Even more than the defenders of isolationism and of extreme individualism, the American proponents of such a position gain plausibility by appeal to tradition. They look for support to our own past history and to the pronouncements of leading statesmen since the inception of the Republic. By reason of our search for insulation from the interventions of European powers and from infection by the disturbances of European rivalries and conflicts, our responsible statesman early emphasized the special interests of the American nation and the American people. The situation of this country as a new state, and widespread awareness among our first leaders of potentialities for development not available to European peoples, actually caused the concept of national interest to be developed and defended as a basis of policy dependent on representative politics some time before the fight for national independence of peoples had become a major theme in European history. National interests were of course pursued by European states. They were indeed pursued both consciously and ruthlessly. But, until the French Revolution, those interests were in most parts of Europe identified with the interests of ruling monarchs. They were likewise formulated and pursued by them, or by ministers dependent on them. At the very most, the national interest was the interest of a limited ruling class. In any event, there was little need to debate, to defend, or to popularize the concept; or even formally to state it. Its identification with the interests of rulers, and the assumption that in that sense it would be followed, were among the things taken for granted. By contrast, the American formulation of the concept, deliberate and self-conscious, was in essence a work of political education. It was a defense of moral principle on the ground that American institutions, based on freedom and necessitating freedom, were at once ethically superior and, vis-à-vis other nations, precarious.

Subsequent to the French Revolution, the moral equivalent of the American idea of national interest emerged as the right of national self-determination. In essence it signified a revolt against alien monarchies which combined arbitrariness in government with control over peoples not their own, a control achieved either by dynastic alliances or by conquest. In what it combatted, that aspiration, so close to our own concept of national interest although developed under different and lastingly difficult conditions, was in intent and initiation liberating and moral. But in the course of time it was in many areas transformed into an aggressive and integral nationalism, whose principles were exclusion and superiority rather than peculiar contributions to a common good based on a theory of comparative cultural advantage. Yet the European development and debasement of nationalism took well over a century. The pristine ideal was belatedly espoused and defended after the First World War by Woodrow Wilson, who envisaged it on the American analogy and experience. Nevertheless, even today the aspirations to national freedom from alien oppression by many peoples of Europe have not been realized. After brief freedom, they have fallen behind the Iron Curtain. They have become satellites, and virtual subjects, of the Soviet Union. But by now it is also obvious that European peoples cannot achieve national independence on the basis of unlimited national sovereignty. The concept of national interest as exclusive, and backed by power politics, leads only to disaster. The facts of political and economic geography force recognition that national well-being and national freedom necessitate interdependence and an acceptance of national interest as supernational. Recent steps towards European union indicate awareness of the situation and a growing willingness to bow more or less gracefully to its imperatives.

European nations are incapable of achieving material well-being in unsplendid isolation from one another, quite apart from the threat to their political independence which arises from Russian power. Manifest weakness therefore slowly forces them towards the limited supernationalism of European union as their real interest. On this side of the Atlantic, the vast strength, developed resources, and higher standard of living of the United States makes a policy of narrow national interest for its people unnecessary, inappropriate, and harmful. The very conspicuousness of our position necessitates the adoption of a far broader internationalism as national interest. Otherwise envy elsewhere will generate a united power of which we are the intended, and, soon or late, will be the actual, victim.

In Europe the ideal of national self-determination is static and anachronistic. There is no necessity or justification for possession of full national sovereignty. Exclusive national responsibility for self-protection and for all required public activities on behalf of the people's well-being is impractical. The ideal of American national interest as insulation from the rest of the world in order to develop and protect our vast territory and our morally superior institutions is no less out of date. In Europe and America alike, ideals of independence without interdependence are today morally stultifying. The achievement of the very purposes envisaged and pursued in an earlier period through attachment to those ideals today necessitates their abandonment. In Europe the requisite substitute is at the minimum a limited economic and military union. Our own imperative is international leadership through extension of our own principles of political society.

The current advocacy of an exclusive national self-interest, which is to be pursued and furthered by a callous realism based on what others must for the moment accept and we may successfully impose, has no relation to the original American concept of national interest. Rather, it is a witting or unwitting attempt to apply to and impose on our people alien dogmas drawn from political thought current in Europe during the latter part of the nineteenth century. Those dogmas were, indeed, grounded in Europe's long-lived political institutions. But they ultimately led to policies disastrous alike for the nations of that continent and to its whole culture and civilization.

From the French Revolution on, European countries had taken over or continued the tradition of monarchical sovereignty and absolutism even where their national independence was begotten of revolt. Continuing or newly created monarchical régimes were likewise infected by the new nationalism. Nationalism was at the outset conceived as at once liberation for particular peoples and as a means to the service and enrichment of humanity. It was soon transformed into a self-conscious awareness of the lack of mutual interests shared with others, and a sense on the part of each nation of superiority to its neighbors. Indeed, the very struggle for national emancipation and the very attempts to achieve national self-consciousness begot such emphasis. For they necessitated stress on opposition and apartness, the cultivation of peculiarities of national character, and sensitiveness as to the distinctive achievements, or frustrated potentialities, of particular peoples. The need to stress difference and to fight other nations in order to gain political freedom made it easy to forget that the nation was a part of humanity and gained its justification from its contribution to a shared culture. Absence of restraint on a nation's self-directed functioning and development was justifiable insofar as it created conditions whereby a people could enrich and diversify the cultural stock of humanity. But cultural nationalism was frequently perverted into a nurturing of resentment against alien governors. It became the seed-bed of planned revolt and a confession of present political impotence for which it was itself inadequate compensation. In any event, nationalism was duly transformed into a minimal claim to a sovereignty which included freedom to conduct foreign affairs on a basis of particularity and denial of an international law grounded in common reason. Its maximum, and more nearly ideal, pretension was to a complete superiority over other nations. Such superiority normally involved a concomitant obligation to attain and use power in order to expand. To rule other neighboring peoples and to gain territories and subject populations on other continents was testimony to the nation's greatness. Such greatness had to be achieved without regard to economic profit or loss, though supposed opportunities to acquire needed resources or outlets for surplus population provided a convenient rationale for aggression and expansion.

Positivist sovereignty and balance of power

New political theory both preceded and promoted this development and was in turn reinforced and rendered more extravagant and extreme by it. Again, the foundations had been laid in the earlier period of royal absolutism, through the development of the modern doctrine of unlimited sovereignty, as opposed to its more moderate medieval counterpart. Nevertheless, in its genesis that doctrine was an attempt to achieve efficacious order both internally within the nation and internationally. Monarchs were in fact uncontrolled. They could be rendered moral only by emphasis on their exclusive responsibility for the well-being of their own people. They had a duty to maintain an international order which embodied moral principle. They could assure the prevalence of such principle by pursuing policies grounded in enlightened self-interest and expediency. The task of teaching them their international obligation and of providing them with the needed rationale was undertaken by Hugo Grotius, as the internal one was the work of Jean Bodin. Grotius was one of the great natural law theorists. He was the founder of an international law which related secular interest to Protestant insight in the light of reason. He espoused a doctrine of monarchical sovereignty as a sanction for a law of nations which had its source in the mutual interests of nations, and was directed to the universal good of humanity. That sovereignty was not a proclamation of the irresponsible ruler or of the exclusive particularity and unrestrained self-interest of national peoples. Nor did it become so transformed till at least the end of the eighteenth century, though already in the seventeenth John Locke unwittingly opened the flood gates, since he constitutionalized power only within the nation and not between nations. The eighteenth-century natural-law thinkers in general overemphasized rather than underplayed the element of universal moral and rational principle; though the greatest legal philosopher of the age, Montesquieu, revived and reinterpreted the wise insight of Grotius, whereby he related actual conditions to reasoned and universal principle. Our own Founding Fathers inherited the natural law philosophy. It informed their attitude to international law, and thereby bridled and directed their formulation of the initial idea of an American national interest.

The view that law was purely positive, the product of the state's will alone, achieved both general currency and respectability early in the nineteenth century, thanks to the teachings of the Englishman John Austin. Austin's doctrine of sovereignty was formally propounded as a logically necessary legal postulate for a political society. Nevertheless, in the sphere of relations between states its logic involved a denial that international law was true law. It resulted, consequently, in the reduction of that law to pious aspiration and to legally irrelevant profession of moral principle or intent, without effective restraining force. Austin's own objective was no doubt intellectual clarity. His positivism was intended to aid morality and not to combat it. For it emphasized the gap between actuality and aspiration and made clear the path which must be followed to reach from the one to the other. Yet the popularization of politics and the impact of nationalism led to a different and unintended result. His morally ill-fated but institutionally triumphant doctrine served as an emancipation of governments from ethical restraints in their dealings with foreign affairs, and in their search for imperial expansion. What was proffered as a technique for overcoming an acknowledged limitation on moral aspirations became a justification for unrestraint in dealings between nations and a rationale for power uninformed by principle.

In its own day Austin's teaching constituted a valuable psychological prop to the British theory and practice of balance of power as a means to preserve and further England's national interests. In particular, a stabilized continent was a condition necessary for Britain's own profitable commerce, its unthreatened island security, and its undistracted cultivation of its colonial empire and its world trade. England had conceived of itself as the balance wheel of the European states system much earlier. Indeed, a century previously the first Baron Halifax had systematically propounded that doctrine of the nation's interest, and had related it to naval power. Likewise, after the Napoleonic Wars, Canning had boastfully and inaccurately proclaimed England as the pivot and creator of a far wider balance. For the proclamation was in truth a prophecy, even before Tocqueville's, of a new power on the horizon. That power in due time refused to play the role set for it in Britain's scheme, while it rendered a merely European balance irrelevant, ineffective, and unimportant.

But in the nineteenth century England's European balance of power policy, buttressed by positivism and based on interest, was to a considerable degree effective in maintaining peace. To treat that balance as an immoral practice of power politics unconcerned with a broader welfare is manifestly unwise and unfair, as recent analysts have indeed realized. It was a practice suited to an order marked by sovereignty, by political as well as by legal positivism, and by nationalisms irridentist and integral. For British statesmen attempted by means of yet another hidden hand to relate a particular nation's interests to a broader aspiration to peace and order. They accepted the lack of a true international law which was rationally grounded, universally applicable, and effectively sanctioned. Under the given conditions, they strove to create a moral equivalent for such law. In a world of unenlightened expediency and unstatesmanlike national ambitions, the British practice of balance of power was an attempt by realists to secure through calculating and undogmatic use of their country's own power the nearest available approximation to what a genuine law of nations, grounded in universal moral principle, might have been expected to produce under happier circumstances.

Some of the more moderate among the present proponents of American policy based on realistic calculations of national interest correctly argue that the United States has taken the place as a world power once held by Britain. Today, they rightly insist, we are the leading representative of the Western ethos and aspirations. They note that the British balance of power technique proved successful over a century of more of modern history. They argue that the policy failed in the twentieth century in part because of a decline in that British power which had made it effective. Moreover, it failed also because of the rise of a different ideal of international organization and institutions, first embodied in the League of Nations. After World War I the United States had gained much of the power lost by England. Though it refused to support its own creation by taking a full share of responsibility for its working, America became a main sponsor of the new theory and practice of international relations, conceived in opposition to the balance of power concept. The latter was misunderstood, abused, and rejected as immoral. For unfortunately the liberal's longing for a brave new world was not complemented by any great understanding of the conditions governing statecraft. The resultant change in orientation was largely responsible for the disorders and distresses which culminated in World War II. Yet the lesson was not learned, as United Nations and all related and analogous activities demonstrate. Even patent failure due to Russian ambition and Communist dogmas have hitherto produced no real repentance. We have not returned to a way of conducting foreign affairs whose success has now been doubly demonstrated, by earlier effectiveness first, and by disaster through abandonment subsequently.

Yet the lesson, the balance-of-power advocates insist, is plain. America, possessed of England's sometime power, must also adopt and adapt its concept of policy. It must not naïvely rely on international good will. To hope and strive for a genuine community of interests between nations is futile. For their inequalities render such community impossible and make the search itself delusive. America must acknowledge to itself its own power and must fearlessly use it. It must clearly recognize that an international organization is at best a convenient instrument, and often an impediment. It must be firm in its determination that such organization shall at no time impose restrictions which decrease the efficacy of American policies. The only real alternative is between a narrowly selfish and expansionist use of power, accompanied by delusions of grandeur whose outcome is apt to be defeat, and an enlightened and responsible promotion of the national interest, directed to the sustained husbanding of American leadership through moderation in objective combined with firmness in action. But the latter choice, these advocates tell us, involves the proper selfishness of minimizing risks which could dissipate power. We must speedily become aware that the United States can by deliberate action create and preserve a balance of power in the rest of the world. On the other hand, it cannot impose its will or its way on that world, or over a major part of it. Likewise, it cannot attain security by a callous or indifferent isolation, provocative of envy and resentment. For sooner or later such a course will promote alliances in aggression against it. Rather, under new world conditions and with its own new-found authority it must realistically continue the sound traditional policy of insulation. But today that policy necessitates America's becoming the balance-wheel. In its own and the world's interest in undisturbed peace it must accept the role of moderating arbitrator between powers. Today, this means that we must function as a balance both between systems and between political philosophies.

The conditions of such a venture, its proponents argue, are clear. At the moment we live in a bipolar world. Two powers are arrayed against one another. The one is supported by subject satellites, the other relies on subordinate allies who are nevertheless equal and independent in law, in diplomacy, and in morals. It is America's duty and interest to destroy such bipolarism. It must so organize and encourage its allies, West and East, that they become in effect independent blocs opposed to Russia. Together they will then create a roughly equal power, sufficient to counterbalance that continental country. The United States will be the make-weight in reserve. It will bring its influence and power to bear wherever need be to overcome in those blocs any weakness which might, if uncorrected, allow Russia to gain local preponderance, to expand, to upset the balance, and to re-create a bipolar situation which would result in our having to take more positive action, and perhaps to go to war.

Bipolar conflict and balance of power

Such a position is superficially plausible and appealing. For it avoids the extremes of isolationism and of utopian internationalism. Its adoption would seemingly enable the United States to pursue and protect its particular interests as a nation. On its terms, we could keep at a minimum the costs of defense and reduce to a minimum the likelihood of involvement in war. What is more, in doing these things we should also serve the causes of peace and of freedom of peoples elsewhere. Yet we would be committed to the promotion of no ideology, to no annoying insistence on the superiority of our ways, to no duty either to impose our institutions or to use up our resources in a vain attempt to raise others towards our living standards.

Nevertheless, the policy of balance of power is today impracticable. Its initiation would immediately necessitate the organization and buttressing, if not the creation, of at least one side of the balance. The force to be counterpoised against the U.S.S.R. would have to be brought into existence. In Europe, an old world would have to be called into being by revivification ere the new world could make itself the balancing force. In the Far East, the radically different problem of organizing a modern system of independent and modernized states would present equal difficulties. From the outset, therefore, it is clear that such a program is artificial. It involves a mechanical attempt to manufacture an equivalent of what was in its day a growth of policy out of living political forces and established conditions of international relations. In the name of reliance on historical experience and use of the teachings of history, it overlooks or fails to understand the reality of history as living and changing situations. These necessitate new techniques to implement our lasting moral objectives.

Further, the conditions for a balance of power system are absent, in a more fundamental sense, as is any sincere intention to follow such a policy. For the assumption of the balance-of-power system was that the members of the European states system were agreed on one fundamental, despite all their conflicts: nation-states in general and the overall pattern of those states were there to stay, even though an individual state might be conquered, occupied, and in the extreme case eliminated. Calculations of national interest might dominate policy, and individual states might have ambitions to expand. But no basic differences in philosophy separated the parties involved. No national government felt that it embodied a system of values or a way of life utterly incompatible with those prevalent in its neighbors. Sustained coexistence was never impossible. Nor would the continued existence of one member permanently do outrage to the total philosophy of life of another.

A power which sought to act as the balance-wheel could therefore contemplate the likelihood of having at some time to switch sides, to throw its weight to the support of the other major bloc in the balance. It had to view such action as a genuinely possible future expediency. It had to be convinced that, if and when it was driven to that choice, its action would correct the balance and insure peaceful stability, not undermine the whole system. It would not give aid and comfort to powers fundamentally opposed to its own way of life. For no powers were committed to eliminating all possibility of the continued existence of nation-states with divergent interests and different forms of government and social organization, and to rendering the very idea of a nation-state irrelevant. The balance-of-power system thus involved a certain international agreement on fundamentals. A neighboring state might err and do wrong. But no state or group of states was inherently evil beyond chastisement and beyond redemption short of radical revolution.

By contrast, fundamental irreconcilability is the essence of current bipolar alignment and conflict. However real the national and imperial interests of the U.S.S.R., Communism as a world philosophy and as a way of life to be spread to all societies is that country's basic commitment. It is also the ideological instrument necessary for the effective pursuit of Russia's particular customary ambitions, which on a superficial view appear essentially unchanged.

The facts are indeed recognized. Those who argue that American national interest necessitates a balance-of-power policy do not seriously contemplate a possible future when we should be required to throw our weight to the Russian side. From such a line of action they would quite properly recoil in horror. Moreover, they are no doubt correct in the assumption that within a foreseeable future it is the anti-Communist powers which will need the support of a make-weight. Yet a policy whose defined conditions and enduring consequences would be unacceptable to its own proponents cannot be a proper formulation of national interest, nor a genuine realism. The nature and degree of support which ought to be given to actual or potential opponents of Communist and of Soviet ambition, East or West, are still open to debate. But bipolar opposition and conflict are lasting and fundamental as long as the Soviet Union adheres to neo-Marxist teaching and promotes it as a world program. Hence debate over policy cannot be conducted, nor American interest furthered, on the theory and practice of balance of power.

The nation as real being

A new American balance-of-power system is not, then, a practicable way to further the nation's interests. Its advocacy is not an effective defense of power politics against universalist ethics. Present American emulation of nineteenth-century England is anachronistic. But a more thoroughgoing and direct doctrine of national power and pride derives, consciously or unconsciously, from ideas and policies developed and followed on the Continent, and especially in Germany, during that same period. Its source was Georg Friedrich Hegel, the German Idealist who early in the century developed a philosophy of history and politics which made the evolution of the state the growth of reason and the progressive achievement of God on earth. The state was the very embodiment of right. The individual at heart willed and submitted to its law and commands because his own reason, however shaky, gave him a clear perception of its superior moral nature. Hegel, indeed, envisioned the ultimate possibility of a universal world state. But his immediate purpose, and his influence, was to give support to the nation-state's search for strength. It was the absolute duty of the individual to submit to his state and to identify himself with it without reservation. The state was a real being, and a fully moral one. It was not merely a necessary and convenient instrumentality and institution.

Early in the second half of the nineteenth century this teaching was curiously complemented and buttressed by a Swiss scholar, Johann Caspar Bluntschli, whose study of the principles of politics was to have lasting and international influence for half a century or more. Bluntschli was in his basic viewpoint a defender of universal ethics and an ardent exponent of principled international law. Nevertheless he mixed together the new Darwinian teachings of evolution, which he applied to the state conceived as person, with a revived medieval organismic doctrine, which he restated with an almost medieval quaintness. His dominant concern was, indeed, the relations of church and state, rather than international relations. His ideas were especially related to the Kulturkampf conducted by Bismarck. Where medieval thinkers had turned to astronomy, and endeavored to identify Church and State with sun and moon, or vice versa, according to their predilections, Bluntschli turned to biology. He unhesitatingly found the state male and the church female. He accepted the accepted opinion of his time and place as to the proper relation of authority and subordination between the sexes. His intent was relatively innocuous. Indeed, it was in line with the liberal thought of his day on the issues of secular supremacy. But his doctrine of the state as organism was taken up by other and differently oriented thinkers. It added to the Hegelian concept that the state was a real and rational being the further idea that it was also a real organism. The consequence was further reduction in the status of persons, who became its cells. Similarly other institutions were naturally its submissive subordinates. Any social pluralism based on the genuine institutional independence of functional authority and purpose was eliminated. The plausibility and utility of conceiving the state as a convenient instrumentality of a society were now doubly indicted: biological science confirmed historical reason.

Thirdly, Heinrich von Treitschke completed the process. He was a nationalist historian and a German patriot enamored of the glamor of power. He insisted on the primary duty of the nation to be strong, and selfish in its strength. Domination was its ideal, and weakness its worst sin. Machiavellian diplomacy was its proper instrument and behavior; military might and the will to use it were its sanctions and assurances of respect and of success. The state might almost be said to exist for international politics, pursued in the national interest. Other purposes were subordinate and instrumental, and the welfare of the nation's citizens was incidental. Politics was a matter of competition between nations. Their purpose was to maintain and increase their own power. Failure was the mark of political incompetence and weakness, and a just doom. Success was justification. To talk of higher ethical objectives at home or abroad was idle and nonsensical prattle. The nation was reason and highest organism. The relations of nation-states were a Hobbesian war of all against all, whether the fight was overt or covert.

This collection of ideas, expressed in varying forms and with different emphases by many thinkers in many lands, may be summed up simply. The nation is a real being to which persons must be sacrificed. It is a final unit in the world's order. Its interests are particular: they are not reconcilable with those of other nations save through temporary expediencies and force or the fear of force. Its policies must be based on considerations of gain and loss of power, on calculations of available power and of the consequences of various choices in its use. Power itself is men and resources, propaganda and morale, as these can actually be organized and applied to generate, and if need be to use, force. In their totality, these ideas have generally been associated with strong, or autocratic, governments. In recent times they have been extravagantly overstated and ruthlessly followed by dictatorships.

In democracies, the emphasis on the real national being and the crude reduction to unimportance of the individual have not proved possible. Nevertheless, in crisis the content of appeals to loyalty, and for patriotic sacrifice, have often revealed the unconscious and latent presence and influence of such concepts. The danger of attributing real being to the state is, however, hidden. For the appeal for hard-headed realism in the realm of international strategy seems initially to rest on ample empirical evidence of the behavior of governments and peoples. Actual practice gives plausible support to the conviction that in international relations it is necessary to be Machiavellian. Likewise, it gives seeming empirical support to the idea of real national being. For nation-states are the obvious, as well as the legal, units of world politics. Hence the serious harm to persons which follows from turning a convenient abstraction into a superior entity possessed of independent purposes escape notice. Rather, a false concept of the nation gains support on the most down-to-earth and pragmatic considerations, which appeal to persons utterly impatient with high-flown ideology.

Realpolitik as American policy

That such seemingly alien ideals should today find expression and acceptance in the United States is therefore in no way astonishing. On their face, such viewpoints utilize an integrating and unifying doctrine of national interest as a ground and support for sensible and practicable policies. For America does possess vast power and wealth. Yet our past strivings to achieve a better world on the basis of an ethic which transcends nationalism have not proved notably successful. Many of our citizens have experienced a deep disenchantment with the naïve and fruitless liberal internationalism of only yesterday. They have also been shocked by what they regard as conspicuous uncertainties, errors, and failures in our diplomacy and foreign policy.

Moreover, we have never completely lost sight of the initial doctrine of national interest propounded by some of the Founding Fathers. That element in our tradition facilitates the acceptance of a harsher European doctrine of the nation, once the latter can be made to appear consonant with democratic convictions and aspirations. To that end they have simply to be cleansed of their autocratic and totalitarian connotations and of arrogantly imperialist and expansionist overtones.

Hitherto, indeed, this country has consistently rejected the European pattern of the state marked by sovereignty or possessed of real being. It has avoided integral nationalism. Nevertheless, the idea of the nation which developed out of the Civil War experience and the struggle against disruption, the later impact of German concepts of state and nation in the days of German scholarship in America, and the more recent fact and necessity of wide powers in the hands of the federal government—these have together created attitudes not utterly unfavorable to such viewpoints and policies. Distress and anger at an obvious cynical realism in the conduct and policies of the Soviet Union have combined with the undeniable successes achieved by its forceful sponsorship of Communism to give further warrant to the power politics thesis. It seems necessary to fight fire with fire. The lasting and nerve-racking tension of bipolar conflict encourages the belief that war is inevitable. Its course will necessitate total devotion of resources and complete unity of attitude if victory is to be achieved. Since war is force applied, the real considerations are how to create such force speedily and sufficiently, and when to bring it to bear. It is possible to generate so great a force that the would-be aggressor will be cowed into abandonment of any desire to risk the arbitrament of war. Russia may then give up any possible intent to attack our shores or demolish our cities. It may even hesitate to attack or invade other lands where we have shown a clear interest in their unmolested freedom, and have revealed our own intention both to support by force those who are attacked and to defeat the forces and destroy the régime of the aggressor.

The Russian rulers may, however, be unable to back down without ruinous loss of prestige abroad and possible loss of power at home. They may be driven by compulsive necessity to compete with us in armaments, and to use subversive propaganda here and in other non-Communist countries. Under such circumstances formal peace is sustainedly precarious, and real peace unattainable. We ourselves will then be lastingly unable to enjoy the benefits of a sane world in calm security. Given such a prospect, it might be desirable for us to force the issue and to make defensively aggressive war at a time and place of our own choosing.

In any event, our enemies not less than our professed friends of the moment are concerned only with their own interests and chances as nations. They will be impressed and influenced solely by our demonstrated national unity, our possession of might, and our will to use force if and when necessary for the protection and furtherance of our own interests as a people.

Such, broadly, is the line of argument put forward by American analysts who see little promise or profit in any policy not rooted in tough-minded national self-interest and ruthless response to ruthless men. Accordingly, they have espoused *Realpolitik* as a proper philosophy for American democracy in its dealing with foreign affairs.

Such insistence that we must shape our policies on an informed awareness of conditions and attitudes prevalent elsewhere is indeed nothing new. Nor is it in any way sinister: a merely *a priori* and deductive politics, internal or international, is pure folly. It is important for the government of this country to know the conditions, needs, motives, judgments, and attitudes prevalent in other nations and among their rulers. We must ourselves be clear as to what we want and why. We must then assess our abilities to attain our ends. We must thereupon select the appropriate techniques in the light of the total situation and of all the relevant international relationships.

Such procedure is common sense. Its detailed statement would be boringly pointless platitude were it not for the strange appeal of the idea that enunciation of high moral aspirations is enough. Yet misguided idealists do hold that noble sentiments are self-effectuating because, moving from heart to heart, they move men to demand, and governments to carry out, right actions in all their specific detail. This last idea is, moreover, often supplemented by another, which is still stranger and formally irreconcilable with the first: to indulge in the negotiations of diplomacy and international politics is itself corrupt and corrupting. For the goods sought are ultimately and necessarily moral, as true goods must be by nature and definition. It is therefore improper to use political techniques, the arts of imperfection, for political purposes. At its best this argument rests on the thesis that no good can be achieved in international relations without a prior change of heart and a broadening of horizons. That statement is correct as an observation that peoples or rulers who are convinced of their superiority and of their duty to pursue exclusive national interest will be unlikely to promote peace and the world's general welfare. It is preposterous insofar as it implies a moratorium on international relations unless and until a campaign of moral conversion has been successfully conducted. Then indeed all men would think and behave as ideal, rather than merely actual, brothers. But then, too, all politics would cease to be necessary.

The realist's contrary insistence that the nature and conditions of politics are inherently no different in international than in internal affairs is a wholesome protest against the view that foreign affairs are merely sinister conspiracies. It is also a proper warning that diplomacy cannot be evangelical revivalism. But a more recent and strident realism has at once falsified the American concepts of state and nation and has unwisely belittled moral principles as a fulcrum in international affairs and a source of American national power.

This latter viewpoint has its origins in a correct realism. It starts from an awareness of the imperfections of men and of the necessity for politics. It develops out of a disgusted distaste for men of good will who render themselves impotent and their aspirations ineffective by their own abhorrence of their unsaved fellows. But the positive argument claims and denies too much. It states that American policy based on advocacy and espousal of moral purposes necessarily becomes weak and bland. Such policy encourages self-delusion at home. Yet the purpose of international politics is the defense and furtherance of the national self-interest in a world of competing powers. Their interests are not and cannot be consonant. Concern for the interests of others is not this nation's business, but theirs. They know those interests. They are responsible for their furtherance. They will work to further them. They will exploit to their own advantage any American altruism. They will not be grateful for any help we give them. They may even resent it just because it emphasizes the extent of our power and wealth. As to an overriding world interest, that is pure delusion. The inequalities of condition, the diversities of culture, and the differences in mores of the peoples who inhabit and divide the globe make even a statement of its contents and conditions well-nigh impossible. Seriously to work towards the creation of one world is as a present national policy futile and wasteful, even if we recognize that its achievement lies long in the future. A sincere intention to maintain American institutions and standards against any pressure to level downward does not excuse the folly of loose commitment to vague plans for uncertain ends. At the most, the new realists argue, professions of high and altruistic moral purpose may have value as propaganda. They may effectively aid in the promotion of national interest insofar as they win friends or embarrass and weaken enemies. Even then, there is need for care not to delude or mislead our own people, who control political power; or their responsible servants, who formulate and execute policy.

Once the advocates of *Realpolitik* make even so modest an admission, they give away the case for eschewing moral considerations in the formulation and conduct of policy. For, once it is made, the view that moral principle weakens or is opposed to realistic power politics has to be abandoned. In intent, the admission may be simply an assertion that an ignorant, unreflective, and uncalculating rank-and-file abroad can be deluded by our moral professions to our advantage and their loss. Nevertheless, the implication is that moral principle has some force in the world. But if it does, there are common concerns and aspirations which motivate men beyond selfish particular interests, and even against them.

The errors in "national interest"

A realistic examination of recent international politics conducted on realist premises indicates that the profession of universally applicable moral principle is vital to the generation of national power and influence. Hypocrisy in such professions is a source of weakness, rather than of strength. Likewise, our sincere adoption of a principle of exclusion and superiority would be a fundamental weakness. It is not to be offset by force. It is ultimately fatal just because the peoples of the world have a real commitment to the opposite ideal. Their interest in that principle combines with their own narrower national interest to create opposition to any power whose profession and practice is merely selfish. On this point, the general reaction of the Western world to Nazism and Fascism should be sufficient testimony. That reaction was indeed long delayed by a decent incredulity. But in due time the professed realism of the totalitarians proved unrealistic both on its own premise of success as criterion of truth and on the correct claim that such success is proof of power.

Wartime Japan and present-day Russia both offer striking testimony on the more general issue of morals in politics. The Japanese doctrine of a Co-Prosperity Sphere was less than universal in its address and appeal. Yet it was not narrowly particularistic. Japan proclaimed itself champion of a common interest among Asiatic peoples, grounded in the ideals of freedom and equality. Thereby it created over a large area a widespread welcoming consent to its leadership. The initial conviction that Japan intended to work for a cause beyond its exclusive national interest generated power in support of its expansion. But revelation that the Co-Prosperity doctrine was spurious and was intended only to further the domination of Japan and the subordination to it of other Asiatic peoples came speedily and was conspicuous. It quickly diminished the ardor of those peoples, and begot their resentment. The consequent state of mind and spirit materially aided America's work in gaining victory, especially since we promised a different dispensation and gave evidences that the promise was sincere.

Of late the nationalistic and imperialistic motives of the Soviet Union have likewise become increasingly clear. Its communist professions, however initially sincere, have been progressively corrupted. Its attempts to achieve the communist ideal have been virtually abandoned or indefinitely postponed, at home, in satellite countries, and even in China. Signs of resentment, of a desire by some of its citizens and subjects to escape, and of diminished positive morale are slowly becoming evident, even though they give no warrant for naïve hopes of revolution or of easy collapse under attack.

Moreover, it has for long been manifest that the international power of Russia and the spread of its influence, both in the Western world and in the Far and Near East, have rested on the universalistic moral principles derived from Marx, and on the promise of social justice and equality contained in his teaching. Granted all the errors in Marxist philosophy, his moral doctrine has had an enormous appeal. It has generated and spread the power of Russia as the custodian and missionary of his principles. Hence Russia's subsequent realistic power politics has enabled some peoples, once impressed by its promise, to call a halt and to stem the tide. They have been aided in that course by the alternative moral teaching of democracy. The Russian profession of "people's democracy" has itself been further testimony to its leaders' own realistic awareness of the power of democratic moral principle. The new theory has constituted an attempt to offset the consequences of Russian ruthlessness, and to distract attention from the true nature of its order. By that doctrine Russia gives recognition to the strength of its opponent's case, which does not rest on a narrowed realism.

The force of that case is unwittingly and unintentionally weakened by the realist's falsification of the nature and practice of American institutions, by a consequent betrayal of the moral purpose they embody, and by a resultant diminution of the power which they are thereby able to create. For the realist puts primary emphasis on the forceful power which the nation can generate and use in its dealings with other nations. As a consequence, he tends to conceive the nation monistically, as one unit in concept, in thought, and in action. Almost inevitably he lapses into the idea that it is a real and organic being, even when he does not deliberately adopt the viewpoints of political idealism and organicism. At a minimum, he holds that the nation is endowed with a monistic sovereignty. As American, he does indeed accept the democratic idea. But he conceives of democracy in narrowly political terms. He deplores the cross-purposes of pressure groups insofar as these lead to a lack of neat and sustained pattern in the formulation and carrying out of policy. He deems it the major purpose of politics, canalized through government, to achieve and impose a single and overriding idea of national interest. The very emphasis on realistic considerations of power combines with the attribution of primacy to foreign affairs, where power is demonstrated, used, and tested, to beget a statist attitude and to promote statism. The emergency powers of government and the unity of loyalty and commitment characteristic of crisis and war tend to become the ideal of national politics. For they express an ultimate national interest, even though its positive content is slight. They reveal an undisturbed national coherence. They lead to a clear and sustained pattern of action.

The unintended result of such doctrine is both ironic and paradoxical. The point of departure is concern for the national interest and a desire not to sacrifice that interest in supposed service to others. The intent is to further and strengthen national institutions; to husband national wealth and maintain national standards of living; to preserve the particular patterns of national culture; and to avoid that leveling downward and the drab uniformity supposed to result from a thorough internationalism, which is in any event held impracticable and delusive. Yet the outcome is to sacrifice or limit those liberties and that concern for rich variety in instrumental goods and in ultimate cultural interests which have been the special mark and achievement of the American adventure and have constituted the very bases of resistance to European concepts of state, of sovereignty, and of the integral nation. In the name of national interest based on national power, foreign affairs are given primary consideration. Domestic affairs are subordinated and subject to unusual controls on the ground that the nation is a unit competing for strength and safety in the world. As a consequence the persons whose furtherance and betterment are the professed purposes of policy are sacrificed and subordinated.

Many people no doubt support and consent to such a position by reason of distress at the disturbance of normal ways of life consequent on bipolar tension. They resent distraction from undisturbed enjoyment of the blessings made possible by democracy and industrialism in America. Their exasperation is in large degree begotten of insecurity and uncertainty. In its turn, it begets a patriotic nationalism and a resentment against the U.S.S.R., the disturber of psychological as of political peace. The frantic drive to impose loyalty and to insist on public professions of loyalty necessarily follow. Citizens huddle together aggressively in what is in fact the beginning of an escape from freedom. Simultaneously, their awareness of the nation's wealth and power and of its position of leadership encourages an aggressive pride and a submissive identification with it. These attitudes in turn complement and provide wider range to the fears consequent on insecurity. As a result, by giving a rationale to these impulses and attitudes, the doctrine of a realistic national interest which is to be furthered through power politics tends to become a self-fulfilling prophecy.

National interest as international

The consequence of such developments is both to diminish the effective power of the political nation and to sacrifice our traditional interests as a social nation under the guise of protecting them. Those interests are rooted in moral principles. They are embodied in institutions. They embrace a method which can generate power because they have appeal and offer promise to other peoples. For the lasting American insight and aspiration is antistatist, pluralistic, and a defense of the ultimacy of the person. Our values are liberty with and through equality. Our political method is constitutional democracy. Our preferred social technique is the voluntary association. Our overall commitment is to the social nation wherein interests are compounded and expressed under governments as needful and useful instrumentalities, rather than subordinated to the nation as super-being. The maintenance and strength of that way of life are vital to our own well-being. They are the basis for a propaganda which creates power and support in the world by reflecting our actual practice and purpose. They help persuade others that our offer to help them to achieve a like way is genuine.

The superiority of our appeal in comparison with Soviet Communism rests on such teachings. For Communism also makes a universal promise. But Soviet effectiveness is limited by revelation of Russia's realistic self-interest and its absence of genuine concern for human freedom. Our own strength and the furtherance of our interest as a nation are therefore promoted by an equally positive and universal promise without the Soviet drawbacks. The implication is clear: we must protect and preserve our national interest by an insurance of the safety of our institutionally embodied insights. In order to achieve such a purpose, we must reject the theory and practice of national self-interest based on the view that world political society is composed of nations which are simply struggling units; that each component nation speaks with one voice and is reducible to a rigid unity; and that each is concerned only to generate the power of ultimate force for the conduct of inevitable conflict. We must espouse the positive doctrine that national interests are international. We must become aware that the dynamo which generates power is ethical appeal. We must rest our propaganda for leadership on a genuine solicitude for national differences as well as for shared aspirations. We must avoid the naïveté of word for deed. We must reject utterly any doctrine of American exclusiveness in interest and in international action.

Today the chief impediment to such a policy is the currently prevalent doctrine of national self-interest. That doctrine undermines and sacrifices interests within the nation and the values of the American way of life to a false national unity. It makes the nation a creature and victim of the internecine strife of an international order whose members are puppets. It fails to make American foreign policy a continuation, a projection, and a fulfillment of those ethical purposes which Americans have long professed and pursued. It fails to acknowledge or assert that in the present interconnected world we can continue effectively to pursue those purposes only by sharing them and extending their reach.

It is America's special mission, as it is our one hope for sustained enjoyment of our way of life, to champion in the world the lasting ethical insights of the Western tradition. We must combat their heretical perversion by Communism. We must struggle against their perverse, unintentional, and unrecognized abandonment by the nation-states of Western Europe. Our first obligation then becomes not to abandon them ourselves. At the very moment when the attainment of power offers us the opportunity to achieve and spread our best insights, we must at all costs avoid the European errors in political thought and practice which for well-nigh two centuries we have courageously combatted and forthrightly rejected.

V

The nature
of America's interests

The underlying principles

Isolationism, individualism and legalism, and the idea of an exclusive national interest as bases for America foreign policy all have seeming warrant in our past. Yet they all involve some misinterpretation of that past, and in the present they betray the underlying principles which we inherited from the culture of the West and have striven to realize by the aid of a generous environment and of liberating institutions happily consonant with its reach and variety. To those principles we must remain true at home. From them alone we can derive policies in dealing with others which will render our whole enterprise as a social nation, wherein government is a useful servant, a coherent whole. Only so can we be secure at home while being supported and accepted as leader by all freedom-loving peoples abroad.

By tradition and moral principle alike, the true national interest of the American people is to cherish and further within a protecting governmental and legal order all those specific interests and groups which contribute to the making and vitality of the social nation. They, and Whitman's individual person, who is the ultimate concern and beneficiary both of the public order and of voluntary associations, are under our system alike protected by rights, which themselves must be appropriately defined to meet modern needs. The objectives of our society are to maximize the amount and variety of available consumer goods; to maximize the release of men's energies in producing them and to insure personal satisfactions in the process; and, finally, to provide the highest possible development and enjoyment of the moral, spiritual, and aesthetic capacities of all our members.

Such a statement of objectives constitutes a definition of the real national interest. On that definition, that interest is manifestly in its principles universal, and in practice cannot be realized by parochial narrowness, by selfish exclusiveness, or by a power which relies on force as its primary instrument. Success in struggles between Powers, and the achievement of ascendancy among them through fear and compulsion, are not America's interest as a people. Rather, we must offer and freely export to others our own values, and, insofar as we may, means to pursue and realize them, without any attempt at imposition. We must bid for world leadership on the ground that we represent a moral order and purpose which, by reason of its own binding logic, imposes no dogma and demands no conformity beyond commitment to the method of freedom.

The American view of the purposes of man in society is unique in its devising of suitable institutions for their pursuit and implementation. It necessitates an approach to foreign affairs which reflects that uniqueness. By implication, it defines our principled overall purpose in international relations. It makes the American national interest essentially international. Thus the American view of life not only permits but positively necessitates the unifying of internal and international principles of policy.

The present strength, the vast power, the potential force of this country are all clear enough. By the mere fact of its power, the United States is bound to be of major concern to others in making their own calculations, in formulating their own goals, and in pursuing their own interests. Their concern is independent of our intent to give or not to give material and moral leadership in the world, or to any parts of it. But the conditions of modern interdependence make a Shangri-La isolation on our part impossible, since it cannot be achieved by the unilateral action of a power desiring it. While weak nations confront ambition, a strong one faces envy. Nor is it today possible to leave a major area of international activities to the chance vagaries and the chancy involvements of individual economic judgment and action. Even a narrow expediency and the simplest concern for a sustained though rudimentary safety make a positive and participating foreign policy a necessary part of our politics. The probable impact of happenings elsewhere is an inevitable consideration in the overall conduct of our public and private lives. If we desire to avoid statism at home and to seek and ensue our purposes both there and abroad, we must reject the concept of national interest as the national power of an organismic or idealist state engaged in a struggle for success through triumph by means of power politics.

The ideas of a public order limited by rights and devoted to their protection, of a social order flourishing under their aegis, and of persons as the final and proper beneficiaries of both, allow us to avoid these various ills. In their light, we may develop foreign policies which permit and encourage flexibility and expediency without abandoning principle, which we shall use as criterion and as selector among alternatives. Since our national interest is to preserve and develop the fluid social nation at home, while the principles on which our nation rests are of universal applicability, our international interest is to preserve and further those principles in the world. Such furtherance is also a condition of safety for our institutions and mores in their own homeland. It is likewise an inner moral compulsion. Otherwise our institutions will wither from spiritual atrophy and lack of positive idealism, quite apart from any harm to be done them by possible military attacks on our shores. Happily, however, our own commitment to variety and openness permits recognition and respect for diversities of situation, of institutions, and of aspirations elsewhere. In selling our view and way of life, we are not driven to impose a rigid dogma and to export an institutional straitjacket.

The international interest of the American social nation is a generous and humane tolerance which encourages and aids other peoples to their own development. It supports genuine cultural nationalism. It combats only that perversion of national distinctiveness known as integral nationalism, whereunder the nation-state seeks to embrace and absorb in its service all persons and all associations which function within its territory. For such nationalism normally rests on force, and is always hostile to free variety. The leaders of the integral nation use force to achieve an artificial unity at home, and to impose their dogma and their control on other peoples abroad. By contrast, the sole limits on our own tolerance result from our commitment to the method of freedom. That commitment compels us to combat all types of totalitarian tyranny, by ideological warfare when possible, by force when necessary. It requires a refusal to ally ourselves with such régimes; a deliberate resistance to their expansion; and, under certain conditions, even an intervention in their own lands to prevent oppression by them and to aid in their overthrow or transformation. Our own basic concept of the ultimacy of personality makes it impossible for us to approve the policies, the leaders, or the deliberate supporters of such régimes. Our purpose, in unyielding opposition to them, is to promote the conversion, the liberation, and the welfare of their peoples, whom we recognize as beings possessed both of general human and of specific national endowments and heritages. As a nation, our principle of international interest is not power or empire over others, nor enforced hegemony among them. It consists rather in a doctrine of cultural free trade among nations whose basis is a law of comparative cultural advantage. That law is nonetheless real because its content is not neatly definable. Under it, the common stock of humanity is enriched by the full development of the special insights and creative abilities of component national units, which, when unconstrained, improve the world's cultural stock by cross-fertilization.

The American nation social, not political

To insist that our interest as a people is both social and international is not to deny the reality of national interest. It is, rather, to define its nature. National interest is of necessity the inescapable criterion of policy. To argue that politics, internal or international, ought to be conducted in disregard of the national interest or in opposition to it would be nonsensical, and would involve internal contradiction, logical or psychological. But the view which holds that national interest is a purely self-regarding matter and is to be conceived and pursued without respect for other nations is equally erroneous and equally nonsensical. The power and purposes of other peoples should not be treated merely as terms in an equation for our solution, and as of no moral concern to us. Our national interest is not simply to generate power and use force for ends peculiar to ourselves. It is misguided for us to neglect or minimize the interests we share with others, or to look on such sharing as chance and temporary consonance of power objectives only.

Unfortunately, defenders of a narrow realism in foreign policy have tried to monopolize the term "national interest," and to equate it with tough-minded unconcern for the well-being of other peoples. They have used it to combat more generous viewpoints and to attack the proponents of such viewpoints as being careless of the welfare of their own people. What is more, the endeavor has largely succeeded. Power politics is patriotism, and the larger view is either disloyalty or, what may be equally harmful, a utopianism which deprives the nation both of power and of needed morale. That the definition of the nation's interest as moral and international may under present-day conditions prove also more practically serviceable for generating American power and promoting the prestige of leadership is cavalierly ignored.

The teaching of realistic national interest was no doubt begotten of disenchantment with moral abstractions, and with those pietistical platitudes which in the recent past so often accompanied our foreign policy pronouncements. The reaction was as intelligible as it was excessive. But its reality makes it necessary to insist that the idea of national interest is not a specific policy dogma which is the exclusive property of excluding particularists, who treat other peoples as mere means to our own ends. Their desire to rule out any concern for other peoples in the calculation of our material interest gives such narrow nationalists no exclusive claim to a pure and undefiled American loyalty. For the interests of the people of this nation are inescapably international. Hence a properly defined internationalism cannot be the antagonist of a sound theory and practice of our national interest. It must constitute the essential foundation and condition of enlightened policy. We must refuse a monopoly of the term "national interest" to professed realists. We must make clear that the concept of our international interest signifies no lack of concern for American well-being. Rather, it emphasizes the fact that such well-being rests on a positive participation and leadership in world affairs. For the sake of success we cannot, as in morals we should not, treat other nations as means only. We must discover a principle by which to steer between ruthless power politics on the one hand and naïvely utopian unrealism on the other. Success in that undertaking will also eliminate confusion at home. It will eliminate a narrowed and narrowing concept of loyalty. It will prevent and minimize false imputations of disloyalty or disinterest in American welfare.

Since the inception of the Republic, American statesmen have proclaimed that national interest is the firmament on which our foreign policy rests, or ought to rest. When need be, they have urgently insisted on the defense or promotion of that interest. They have likewise debated as to what constitutes its underlying principle, and what specific policies it implies or imposes. Yet until our own day the all too simple idea that national interest was a single dictum, to be formulated and expressed through a monistic and majestic State, has rarely achieved widespread acceptance. Indeed, the paradox is that throughout our long insulationist history we broadly avoided any concept of a national super-being, whereas in this period of avowed internationalist commitment and purpose we are approaching the European view of the nation-state, at least insofar as the conduct of foreign policy is concerned. The development is ironical, since today most European leaders are aware that the worship of the nation-state has proved deleterious to European culture. We have long urged its evil; and we do not today seek to promote European union in order to create a bigger and better nationalist power unit.

Indeed, the American experience gives little warrant, as the great ethical systems give no sanction, to a concept of national interest based on those doctrines which hold that the state is a super-being, whether as the locus of perfected reason or as a quasi-biological super organism. The pursuit of power without regard to purpose, and the embodiment and expression of power in the integral nation, are courses we have lastingly deplored. From the colonial beginnings, and certainly long before the Revolution, many leaders on these shores were critical of monarchy. Indeed, by Puritan doctrine itself they were antimonarchical, whatever their dependence on the throne for the very bases of their legal existence and their territorial rights. The experience of colonial life in thirteen simple colonies carved from a wilderness was inimical to centralization and to a dominantly political loyalty to the state. Later colonial experience with the mother country reinforced these tendencies. The Revolution itself completed the work and fixed an underlying pattern. The defining of national interest as the interest of the state, whether monarchical or the constitutionalized heir of monarchy, became lastingly difficult.

The idea of national interest was indeed developed early in the United States. It has remained a touchstone for the measuring of policy. The reasons are in essence simple. The Founding Fathers were at once revolutionaries and self-made heirs of the doctrine that statesmanship was the appropriate and highest calling of the natural or aristocratic leaders of society. That view had emerged during the Whig Revolution in England. At that time, landed and commercial leaders inherited the major and essential functions once the prerogatives of Divine Right monarchy. They did so by default, and as the culmination of a revolutionary movement which they ended and completed. In due course their heritage was transferred to the colonies. There our Founding Fathers, themselves successful revolutionaries, were driven to organize public power as they sought lasting safety for their creation. They had separated themselves from the country whose legal possession they had been. They were bound to proclaim that, whatever their distinctions and peculiarities, they were a nation-state belonging to the system of states developed by and in Europe from the Peace of Westphalia on. Jefferson stated the position forcefully in the Declaration of Independence. But the new member had to insist on its status. It had its special interests to further within the system. It was the task of our statesmen, having secured our membership, to implement and define those interests by suitable policies. As revolutionaries and republicans welding a whole from separate colonies, they were especially driven to use the concepts of a nation, a national people, and a national interest for organizing purposes, internal not less than international. It is well not to forget that the United States was the first to stress the modern concepts of nationality and national independence. It happily long avoided the European corollary, nationalism, which speedily followed on the national idea proclaimed in the French Revolution, and variously spread, perverted, and inhibited of expression by Napoleon.

The social and geographical facts of American life, even when coupled with distrust of distant political authority and function, did not of themselves prevent our early statesmen from developing a concept of national interest. Indeed, our national government was endowed with exclusive authority in the sphere of foreign affairs just because some recognition of collective interest was imperative. That power in its turn facilitated the public exploration of the nature of that interest by statesmen. Nevertheless, the conditions of our society did inhibit any tendency on the part of ordinary men to conceive of their loyalty and their nationality as primarily political, and oriented towards the federal government. Men as citizens generally met their legal obligations to that government, and where necessary bore arms in furtherance of the nation's policies. Yet their co-operation was sometimes grudging, and the willingness to serve as soldiers was not always overgreat, as the Union leaders discovered in the Civil War. Even in our own day military service remains for most a regrettable, though real, necessity. In the name of national interest it interferes with the normal pursuit of individual interests. The sum of those interests is held ideally to constitute the more appropriate long-term interest of the nation. Further, the original right of the citizen to bear arms, which was publicly conceived as in the national interest because it provided a reservoir of trained men, was in truth doubly antistatist. It rested on fear of professional armies, as well as an unwillingness to rely on them. For such armies were normally instruments of governments which identified national interest with the rulers' conceptions of public power and prestige. The right was supported, secondly, by a popular sense that a citizen body accustomed to use arms was a wholesome check on the possible temptation to government to act oppressively. The people constituted the nation, and any reminder to persons in authority that they would do well not to equate their ambitions with its interests, nor endeavor to make it their pliable instruments, was wholesome.

In general, Americans have rejected outright the idea of a nation as a real super-being, endowed with independent life and interests, as they have well-nigh escaped the European concept of the state. Certainly the idea that men should be sacrificed to the one or the other, or to the two in combination, is repulsive to them; as is the view that public authorities are the primary force in the formulation of concepts of national interest. There have been, it is true, nationalist movements in these United States. But, owing to the absence of equally powerful neighbors, they have been strikingly different from European movements. Also, they have generally been short-lived, and have rarely captured a widespread and deep enthusiasm. Thus the first major movement of this sort after the Constitutional period, our excursion against Mexico, was severely criticized alike by transcendentalists and by interests differently oriented in geography and commerce. It ended with the deepening of sectional conflict and the defection of Calhoun. The nationalism of the Civil War period and after led, it is true, to new constitutional concepts of the nature of the Union. Yet it was less than successful in its attempted introduction of alien ideas of sovereignty and nation-state. Indeed, the very forces supporting the Union were in major part antistatist, individualistic, and voluntaristic in outlook. Later still, the impact of German ideas in the creation of American academic political and social science failed utterly to bring any widespread conversion to the European ideas of state and nation. The most forceful proponents of these alien doctrines were themselves driven by outer circumstances and inner conviction to the defense of liberty, of property, and of enterprise beyond the purview of government or state.

The American regards his government as an instrument designed for his use and convenience. But unlike those Europeans who share this view, he does not attain a simple monistic view of national interest by making the state his central symbol of loyalty and identification. Like Europeans, indeed, he reverences the symbols of the collective public order, such as the flag (to which as youth he has repeatedly pledged allegiance). Yet loyalty to his nation, though real and deep, is little related to the panoply of public life. The occasions when the American thrills to the acts of statesmen because they embody the sense and reveal the majesty of his nation are rare indeed.

It is for such reasons that the American nation may properly be called social, rather than narrowly political. American loyalty tends rather to center around institutions, from the family outward; around regions, sections and scenery, and ways of life; around personal freedom and enterprise; and around neighborliness. These interests may be loosely summed up as the much-vaunted American way of life. For all its varieties of connotation, and despite all abuses committed and narrowly selfish interests defended in its name, that way symbolizes a central core of experience, emotion, and attachment. It is not a statist concept. It is not identified with government. Though it includes our political mores, it is not in feeling political. Yet it symbolizes the fundamental concerns which it is the national interest to protect and promote.

Foreign policies proclaimed or pursued by statesmen are at bottom judged in the national interest when devoted to such protection and furtherance. Hence glory and aggrandizement of the nation-state are not, for Americans, synonymous with national interest. Moreover, because that interest is social rather than political, Americans can look on the state as purely instrumental, yet at the same time admit that their satisfactions, both instrumental and final, can and must come from identification with shared national interests. They can share in national interests without being driven to glorify a super-being whose claim is sacrifice, whose characteristic ultimate instrument is force, and whose essential impact upon its own members is external and impersonal. The point may be made negatively by noting the relative difficulty in this country, as against England and parts of Europe, of associating the basic emotional elements of local attachment—the particular sights and sounds and smells so dear to the poet—with the devotion to political institutions and to sacrifice in furtherance of national policies. The linkage is difficult to accomplish by means of propaganda. Crisis apart, it is rarely made by the individual either unconsciously or by a deliberate act of will.

The peculiar conception of the American self is a product of a long-lived individualism, of local community, of the open horizons associated with the frontier, and of the vast range in place and in ways of living of the American adventure. It reflects, commemorates, and preserves the pluralistic diversity of a variegated environment populated by persons and groups of highly diverse origins and experience. It renders old-world concepts of national interest—with their stress on power politics and balance of power—meaningless and inapplicable to the American situation.

Admittedly the American concept is more imprecise than these. To be useable, it requires continuous redefinition and recompounding. That need makes difficulties for our own and foreign statesmen, as well as for the analyst who seeks for pattern and formula. Nor are those difficulties lessened by the inherent unpredictabilities of our political-governmental system, which are probably at their greatest in the realm of foreign affairs. Yet in the modern world of conscious, awakened, and aspiring peoples such change and imprecision have one great potential advantage: the tying of national interest to fluidity in social theory and practice. True, they may lead to an exclusive selfishness due to our endeavor to preserve the privileges of our way of life, the products of a combination of favorable circumstances and creative energies. But they warrant some hope that America's root concern and its ultimate concept of the national interest may be the spreading and sharing, with all due adaptation and without intolerance, of its societal blessings. They raise some expectation that we may avoid a narrowed and resented search for the magnificence of imperial power, which is always at least a snare, a delusion, and a pointless sacrifice of persons.

In any event, this American idea provides bases for avoiding a naïve utopianism unrelated to our interests and attachments. It likewise escapes the moral corruptions of a power politics whose course is lasting statism on the one hand and repeated tensions beyond peaceful solution on the other. It therefore holds superior promise in a world where world conquest and peaceful isolation are equally delusive aspirations. In the present bipolar world, the alternatives offered to lesser powers are acceptance of a totalitarian statism or alliance with a nation whose social order permits experiment and variety without sacrificing cohesion and commitment to principle. The preservation and furtherance of these institutional patterns are the essential concepts of national interest of the two major powers involved. The root problems of American national interest would seem to be to draw the proper inferences from its own concept, to implement them at home and abroad, and to persuade others alike of the reality and the validity of its position.

Policy as application of America's philosophy

The implications of such an attitude towards politics for our dealings with other peoples are fairly clear. First of all, on our own principles we are enabled to avoid the evils of attempted imposition of our own institutions and of the present content and use of our values on others differently located in place and in the time of their cultural development. Yet we are not thereby driven to an uncritical tolerance and a lack of all discriminations. We may properly maintain the underlying principles of our seeking and of human freedom, even while we show respect for the inevitably changing and varied content of natural law and rights which are the conditions and means to the development of the person in and through organized societies under government. That achievement of a principle of discrimination may seem minor. Yet our whole struggle against totalitarianism, and for a democratic union, has hitherto been grievously lacking in clarity through the absence of a settled basis for distinction between a principled expediency and temporary expedients. We have found it difficult to differentiate between true friends and those foes who do not chance for the moment to be avowed enemies but pose as allies. We have had still greater difficulty in making clear to others that we are aware of the difference. Moreover, our own thinking about foreign affairs, and about our place and mission in the world, has been distorted and confused by lack of such principled differentiation.

Our heritage of moral suspicion of forceful expansion and our condemnation of imperial adventure go back at least as far as transcendentalist criticism of the Mexican War. But a generally critical attitude towards more subtle expansionist tendencies, where force, symbolized by the Marines, was in the background, stems from this century's critics of Caribbean imperialism and so-called dollar diplomacy. Those criticisms were originally grounded in a recognition that economics may be as powerful as politics, and that it indeed constitutes the essence of politics. They were based on the subtle infiltration of doctrines of economic determinism derived ultimately from Marx. But in the course of the years they developed into a more generic and dogmatic suspicion of any attempt to exert influence on other peoples, or to urge them towards our own ways and viewpoints.

At length any suggestion that our ways were superior was looked on askance. We should not have any political and cultural ideas for export except on a positive demand by others. Such a demand was improbable. Our professed superiorities were subjective and relative. Our pride and sense of superiority are not for export. They ought to be purely for home consumption. They should be hidden as far as possible from the rest of the world.

To avoid any false sense of superiority is indeed necessary to American primacy and leadership in a co-partnership of peoples committed to freedom. An impatient withdrawal from the world and an equally impatient, and exasperatedly forceful, intervention and imposition of our ways on its peoples are alike damaging to our true national interest. Yet we must also overcome our inner sense of helpless unworthiness. We must abandon that misguided tolerance which, inspired by the fear of improper pressure on others, can so readily obscure our own light. We must not disguise or destroy the reality of our shared interest in a crusade on behalf of freedom for men and of fluidity in their societies. The errors of vulgar contempt, vulgar unconcern, and vulgar imposition are not to be met by a shamed and shameful withdrawal. In the name of respect for other peoples, we cannot abandon the duty of selective discrimination between allies and enemies. We must make clear our emphatic commitment to the former. To carry out our obligation requires penetrating discrimination and selective action.

In their absence, our persuasion on behalf of democratic values lacks a coherent consistency. Our assurances of purpose and intent fail to carry conviction. Our propaganda stands revealed as expedient lipservice. Others may judge it deliberate hypocrisy, used to support the temporary or lasting interests of our national power. Certainly they will question whether we regard ourselves as morally involved in their fate. They will doubt whether we really hold dear the values which they and we alike profess. In a world of clashing ideologies, we shall therefore fail to generate effective power by propaganda. For high-sounding appeals which are not in line with behavior and manifest intention beget disillusion. Thereby in the long run they encourage desertion to the enemy, whose morale is immediately strengthened and whose cause is aided by recognition and exploitation of our less than candid proclamations.

Russia's own dishonesty is still plausibly hidden by its use of the promise of ultimate good and freedom, which will become reality only after necessary submission and dictatorship. We cannot convincingly expose and combat dishonesty when we fail to follow out our own teaching of freedom in process as a common and shared adventure and achievement. Our own doctrine gives us no plausible grounds for postponement of concern for the well-being of persons. Therefore lack of coherence in our professions and of consonance of word and deed is immediately harmful to our generating power in ideological warfare, which is a battle of professed moral universals. By contrast, the Soviet leaders can on their premises properly argue that delay in achieving higher standards of consumption and liberty for the individual is not only defensible, but inherently necessary. Indeed, it is forced on them and theirs against their will by the very continuance of our own régime and the continuing acceptance in many lands of its wrong values and methods. Unless we can show that our own ideal is as genuine as it is practicable, we lose our great initial advantage of the promise of goods here-now and in process. We ourselves then encourage public escapes from freedom on the part of others. Yet our task and our interest is to get them to support the method of freedom from a conviction that, along with its demand for endurance, it brings present and ever-increasing material and spiritual welfare.

The ethics and politics of intervention

Support of our values neither necessitates nor justifies a busybody's interference in the affairs of other peoples. We must clearly distinguish between the essence of our values and their particular and varied institutional embodiments. We must be aware that other peoples are often severely limited in their attempt to implement the principles they share with us by conditions they cannot readily change. Our values are for export. But their very nature necessitates persuasion and acceptance rather than imposition. It is, however, legitimate and necessary for us to judge others and to determine our policies towards them in the light of their acceptance or rejection of such values. Our material power, and hopes for our help and fears of our enmity, may produce lip-service to those values by others. It is part of the job of our policy-makers and of informed public opinion to assess the honesty of such professions. More particularly, it is the task of the former to watch the trend of performance in other lands. They must discover whether profession and performance are on balance and through time consistent, and they must determine what allowance may properly be made for difficult circumstances and for those occasional lapses from grace of which we ourselves are also on occasion guilty. They must then inform and alert our representatives and ourselves as to the realities behind verbal appearances. As a nation, we may at the outset accept word for deed, in the hope that profession may lead to performance. We may reasonably hope that the desire for approval and the fear of disapproval by ourselves and like-minded allies will result in progressive realization of democratic values. We may seek to strengthen those who seek such realization by our sympathy and encouragement, and by our disapproval of inconsistent behaviors. But performance we may properly require. For us to denounce willful failures, to withdraw assistance when those in authority seem determined to misuse it, and—where the need is clear and the opportunity present—to encourage and endorse local opposition to governments which either do not share or consistently betray those values is not improper intervention.

Indeed, in countries which are genuinely committed to democratic method and purpose, but which are cursed with powerful and dangerous antidemocratic forces and parties, we have a right and an obligation to strengthen and encourage our friends in every way possible and expedient. We are under no obligation to be nonpartisan in the affairs of other peoples where partisanship means support of our own values and furtherance of our moral cause. We have a duty to assist régimes which are in fact or in sincere profession committed to that cause. Indeed, such partisanship properly complements our propaganda to alienate the subjects and citizens of the Soviet régime, of the present Chinese government, and of the satellite nations from their rulers, and to encourage and organize those already alienated and in covert opposition.

How far we should intervene in the politics and use pressure to change the policies of other nations is solely a question of expediency in the service of principle. We may legitimately hesitate to intervene where we are uncertain of the consequences for our own course, though where possible we should consult our friends in other lands as to what is advisable.

Moreover, a major duty of diplomats and of State Department is to find bases for assessment of what the short and long term consequences of various lines of action and inaction will probably be. With all possible aid from technical experts, they must advise our policy-makers on the techniques and timing most likely to bring desired results, and to avoid unnecessary antagonism.

Clearly, it is not our interest to give aid and comfort to enemies of régimes which are our principled allies. We must avoid providing them with opportunities for internal appeal by outraging national pride and irritating the sensitivities of those less powerful than ourselves. In particular, in our dealings with democratic régimes we must be careful not to give countenance to anti-American argument and appeal by heavy-handedness. That caution is above all necessary in dealing with countries governed under multi-party systems. Their politicians are peculiarly eager for advantage and tend to be more than normally irresponsible. Yet our statesmen, aided by our diplomats, have to judge whether temporary alienation and strident denunciation will or will not result in net gains for the democratic cause. They have to determine whether positive support of constitutional governments by word and deed may not in the long run be less costly, morally and materially, than the concession of silent nonintervention when such régimes are threatened by subversive opponents. The making of such decisions lies in the realm of expediency where, however clear one's principles, error is always possible and within limits forgivable.

Our honest commitment to principle, our demonstration that we follow and further it at home, and our disinterested support of it abroad without any attempt on the basis of our own selfish interests to impose our preferences on others may be expected to produce diminished hostility towards us and suspicion of us. They will increase other people's willingness to listen to our advice and to follow it, rather than to regard it as illegitimate interference. It is, indeed, such considerations which make it especially important to define and maintain our rights at home, and to demonstrate our sustained ability to cope with evils and lacks in our society and to promote its own ideal of classlessness. They likewise make clear the proper scope of nonintervention. We must recognize that diversity of mores, of folkways, and of institutions is legitimate and inevitable. We must show that we respect and rejoice in such differences, subject only to the overriding principle of sustained freedom for personality. Even were it possible to define an ideal social order, we ourselves would not have achieved it and, in any event, could not impose it on others. To attempt to do the latter would be absurd. For peoples are shaped and limited by their location, their history, the resources available to them, and their whole culture as a going concern. No commitment to universal values warrants our denying or ignoring this central fact of human experience. From Aristotle through Montesquieu down to our own sociological, anthropological, and psychological insights, awareness of such diversity has at once necessitated defense of the reign of principle and prevented hope for the perfection of man through its full realization.

The expediency of particular interventions is in any event a matter for debate, and of legitimate differences of opinion. We must become fully aware that on occasion intervention is necessary for the maintenance and furtherance of our own larger international interest. We have to reject the long-lived idea that nonintervention is a duty. In international law the doctrine of nonintervention is counterbalanced in part by a generally neglected doctrine of the right of intervention which goes beyond protection of a nation's own citizens or subjects. The former was in its origin a corollary of monarchical sovereignty, itself a means to secure a workable international order of law and to limit the frequency, by limiting the provoking causes, of conflict between states. Nonintervention was a product of monarchical nationalism and of secularism. It helped to avoid conflicts between nations based on religious differences and on the impulse by men in one country to come to the assistance of oppressed coreligionists in another. It was an extension to the international realm of the *politique* doctrine that the earthly interests of a nation should not be sacrificed on behalf of religion. It was at once a proper corollary of the celebrated principle, *cuius regio, eius religio,* that the ruler of a territory determined its religion, and a critical commentary on its inevitable consequences. In our own time it has continued to be a corollary and implication of the doctrine of sovereignty under conditions which necessitate co-operation and reflect interdependence between nations. Yet the root conflict of our time does not involve the danger of destruction of earthly order and well-being by reason of diverse interpretations of the meaning and road to God. Rather, religion itself, and any sound system of ethics based on concern for the person, are alike endangered. Moreover, the doctrine of sovereignty has been divorced from monarchy and from the concept of the ruler's personal responsibility. It has become rooted in positivism, with a total loss of relation to that natural law which it once awkwardly supplemented and implemented.

Under such circumstances the doctrine of nonintervention is triply dangerous. First, it supports the moral irresponsibility of governments and their lack of practical answerability before the court of world opinion for their internal doings and for their treatment of their own citizens. It does so, moreover, at a time when doctrines of real national being and of super-organism, made more dangerous by insecurity and irrationality, have facilitated the reduction of those citizens to subjects. Secondly, it makes difficult and suspect any attempt fully to seek and ensue personal rights on a world scale. For it abets, and is abetted by, a false tolerance, and it buttresses a refusal to face the tragic potential necessity of employing force for the very sake of the survival of right. Thirdly, it weakens effective emphasis on mutual aid between nations by overemphasizing their particular claims to an absolute and unimpeded self-determination. Such self-determination is as ruinous for peoples as for persons when it is used to justify irresponsibility rather than to facilitate cultural development.

As previously noted, the United States has through most of its course rejected the European concepts both of state and of sovereignty. In particular, it has hitherto successfully combatted their more recent perversions. Therefore, on its own historical, institutional, and moral logic, it should be unimpressed by the interpretation of nonintervention as an absolute legal duty, and above all by the translation of it into a supposed moral imperative binding upon this country regardless of circumstances. It is indeed inexpedient to be an interfering busybody, as the counsels of our individualist predilections amply warn. Yet it is unprincipled to remain uninvolved in the face of human suffering and unmoved by the infliction of indignity, as our more generic personalism, our generous humanitarianism, and our practice of group assistance all teach us. Despite our well-grounded objection to collectivism in the planning and control of our economic life, we have espoused and supported the idea of collective responsibility and the practice of collective action internally, within our hemisphere, and latterly in the world. Sometimes, too, we have made considerable sacrifices of immediate interest, have suffered inconvenience, and have borne high costs on the conviction that action by ourselves alone would not be the proper course in dealing with issues of concern both to ourselves and others. Our better logic makes both intervention and nonintervention aspects and expressions of our root interest in free persons and free institutions, with due consideration for the expediencies which at the moment serve those lasting goods. Our deeper concern is that international law be based on natural law. A world of justice can be realized only through the securing of men's natural rights. These are universal, even though, because they are not absolute nor uniform in content, they cannot be secured by imposition from outside without reference to internal limiting conditions. While our doctrine of collective responsibility can on occasion warrant intervention elsewhere, imperfections in other peoples' systems of rights do not *of themselves* give such warrant. But the rejection by dictatorships of all human rights does.

A thorough-going positivist rejection of the precepts of natural law by others, when combined with an actual denial of all rights, creates an actual presumption in favor of intervention. It does so with increased force when the régimes concerned, in order to spread such denials, themselves become aggressive and expansionist. Our normal desire to preserve the lives of our fellow citizens and of others, and our warranted conviction that the arbitrament of force is not the best technique for settling differences between nations, do indeed create an initial presumption against intervention. But there is an answer to that presumption. When men survive only as material creatures and not as moral beings, existence itself loses all significance. We then confront the necessity of choice between grim alternatives. The better course has indeed its corrupting costs. That is part of that tragedy, bitter, ennobling, and inescapable, which is man's earthly lot and the price of his escape from bestiality. The consequences of forceful, armed intervention must indeed be weighed with scrupulously conscientious care. Today especially the ruthlessness of war and the destructiveness of new weapons tend to be undiscriminating and to a large degree unpredictable in scope and impact. The moral and material costs of war to civilization may outweigh all probable gains. At the level of expediency, indeed, it is necessary to take a leaf from the book of Lenin, in this respect statesman-like without reference to Marx. The conditions for successful intervention, as against merely reckless warfare, must be assessed just as he assessed the conditions of successful revolution as against pointless revolt. But such expediential judgment rests on acceptance, and not denial, of a real alternative.

The essential point is that nonintervention must not be given status as an absolute moral duty. The rightful principle of respect for others and for their responsible exercise of freedom must not be corrupted, however unintentionally, into the moral error of ethical indifferentism. As policy, moreover, it is unscrupulously misleading for us to conduct propaganda beamed behind the Iron and Silken Curtains with a view to creating disaffection there and to encouraging attachment to our own principles, which we proclaim as universal ethical insights, unless we are prepared to be consequent. To urge adherence to our way but to refuse assistance and support to those who give it is at once deceitful and cruel. To aid and abet them in opposing or conspiring against their dictators without recognizing that we ourselves may be thereby committed at the appropriate time to more thorough-going action (even if our enemies, harmed in their interests, do not first thrust conflict upon us) is naïveté or cowardice. Who wills the end wills the means—and all the necessary steps en route.

VI

Essential policies, political and economic

America's interest in international rights

America has the duty and the interest to promote a philosophy of man and society and a consequent theory and practice of rights throughout the world. The carrying out of that obligation and the defense of that interest do not involve simply questions of the limits of tolerance of the rulers of other nations. The issue is not merely on what grounds we should support or combat other governments, or when we are justified in an attempt to undermine them. The international interest of the American people also necessitates our defining of rights as international. We must support an appropriate international bill of rights. We must strive to secure its acceptance and ratification by all governments. We must then take steps to insure that it be in fact observed both in the internal life of peoples and in their relations with one another. Such a bill of rights is in its very essence a statement of commitment to the ethics of democracy and the method of freedom. It is, further, an announcement of at least the minimal objectives common to modern political orders which have made such a commitment; and of the minimal claims of persons which governments must respect, protect, and further beyond immediate considerations of power. For such rights are the very basis of stable and morally purposeful power.

On their own premises, supporters of such an international bill of rights must proffer it to all nations for their adherence. But adherence implies obligation. Likewise, it necessitates judgment by others as to whether the obligation has been, is being, or can be, discharged. A government which by word and deed denies the desirability of personal or group rights, the possibility of their present pursuit or maintenance, or their relevance short of ideal utopia, puts itself out of court. It cannot properly adhere. For us to make compromises in the formulation of rights to gain its lip-service, at the sacrifice of creative and principled substance, is folly and betrayal. Rights are not a lasting enjoyment for a perfected order. They are the conditions for continuous development and expression of finite, fallible, and struggling men in orders forever imperfect, where life is a moral adventure. To seek common ground with rulers and régimes which deny that view is a peculiar folly which robs the compromisers of their very *élan* and morale in the struggle against such doctrine, and of their superior appeal. Totalitarian governments which treat men as depersonalized objects and oppress them ruthlessly under the guise of objective necessity and determinism cannot be régimes of law nor adherents to bills of rights, whatever their legal code or their willingness to sign documents.

We must, therefore, reject also the view that, when revision of the United Nations Charter is undertaken, proposed amendments should be assessed according to whether or not they promote the continuance of that organization as a meeting-place for both poles of the bipolar world and a forum for their debate. By now it should be clear that the coming together of representatives of both groups to air a complete lack of meeting of minds can serve no useful or creative purpose unless it be to permit the Soviet bloc, by its own words and actions, to expose its nature to hesitant peoples. Likewise attempted mediation by neutralist countries between our own system and values and the Communist leviathan is both futile and morally muddying. There is no obligation on the part of the free world to provide a world forum for a dishonest and cynical realism which exploits moral aspiration by means of misrepresentation, and without acceptance of the very bases of morality, even though there may be some value to it in a public self-exposure by the Soviet Union and its satellites. To revise the Charter, not less than to devise and promote a bill of rights, on the basis of a shared and positive moral doctrine is no doubt to exclude from membership those governments which rule a major part of humanity. The resultant order of law is then limited in geographical range, as its supporters are morally aggressive in intent. But, while the reach of such a law may at the moment be limited, its substance rests on and expresses general moral principles of universal applicability genuinely held by adherents. The alternative is either a compromise with those principles, which is in truth their abandonment, or mere lip-service to them, which involves a cynical and hypocritical corruption and tarnishing of them. The exclusion of so large a part of humanity from coverage by an international organization genuinely grounded on a theory and practice respectful of the claims of persons and groups is the consequence of refusal by its rulers to permit the extension of the rule of law and rights within their territories and to their peoples. Our own refusal to compromise is a statement of those conditions necessary to sharing in a common humanistic cause which recognizes that men and women everywhere are entitled to respect and consideration as persons. Refusal by others to share with us in our search to maintain such respect and to translate it into a way of social life is profoundly regrettable. Their genuine adherence would manifestly be welcome and has been sought. But for us to put a nominal unity first, where there is no real unity, and tolerantly to welcome intolerant dogmatists who themselves welcome a world organization only as means to organize for forceful overthrow or destruction of major components thereof—this is totally unwarranted. It is incompatible with effective maintenance and furthering of rights, as is tolerance of deliberate subversion and rejection of the method of freedom within our own nation. No temporary gains through the boomeranging of Communist propaganda in a world forum can offset losses in coherent principle—and in positive collective action based on its acceptance.

Efforts to gain adherence to an international bill of rights and agreement to necessary Charter revisions by nondemocratic régimes which are not in the Soviet orbit nor based on Communist principles raise similar problems and invoke the same principles. It is necessary and proper to formulate rights in such a way as to give them maximum appeal, meaning, and relevance for diverse peoples of different intellectual traditions. It is also appropriate to keep in mind those who lack our own long and complex tradition of social and constitutional democracy and who need the intelligibility of essential simplicities. But such formulation does not require compromise with the alien views of those who glorify public abstractions such as state-nation, treat them as super beings, and in the process debase persons. It necessitates, rather, the discovery of the lowest and morally broadest common denominator between all peoples committed to the ultimacy of personality. In such a bill, we need only to avoid prejudicial statements which are merely present or past applications to specific and limiting conditions of the generic principles which underlie rights.

Nevertheless, general statements of rights must vigorously reveal essential human insights and must not remain meaningless platitudes. In order to mean something they must therefore be implemented by a specific content, by concrete guarantees which provide criteria for assessment of the achievement and the intention of any particular régime. Happily, certain rights, such as freedom of expression and of worship, which were sought and partially achieved in the West as the result of struggles over centuries, have become rather generally the immediate aspiration, even when not yet the practice, of freedom-seeking peoples everywhere. Other more positive rights, which are claims to adequate material conditions and opportunities made possible by the Western industrial order, are at present among the remoter aspirations rather than the immediate practicabilities for nonindustrialized peoples. The defining of acceptable and operable specific rights is therefore an exceedingly difficult task. Nevertheless, it is possible to state the conditions for the general liberation of the individual, even though their achievement may have to be gradual, especially in situations where men must devote most of their energies to the production of instrumental goods. Where circumstances constrain rights in action, many rights have to be modified. Or, to put it otherwise, our insistence that rights be meaningful, and not on the books only, must include an informed assessment of intent, direction, and accomplishment by régimes which are prevented through inevitable circumstances from realization of the best and fullest contemporary achievement. Weaknesses in attitude and failures in performance may necessitate admonition, encouragement, and assistance. Distance from the best practice and realization of rights due to absence of adequate means is itself a potent criterion for measuring the possibilities of assistance programs by more advanced and fortunate nations, and for their knowing their own obligation and enlightened interest. But temporary invincible impotence to attain rights on the part of some peoples is no ground for not including in an international bill of rights all the necessary guarantees and insurances for the pursuit of the good life.

Far less should we compromise principle to placate those régimes unconcerned with the attainment of rights or hostile to the very concept. Adjustments in measuring practice based on our recognition of the difficult heritage or weak means possessed by some peoples is expedient application of principle. Such expediency is necessary in politics. It is, moreover, at once magnanimous and soundly realistic. But there is no need for us to imply that failure to achieve the full scope of needful rights is an inherently satisfactory situation. Nor need we ourselves endorse the watering down of the content of rights at the point of initial formulation. A very limited achievement of rights may in some areas be all that we can properly expect. In such a case, it would be unjust to blame governments for not granting or guaranteeing more. It would also be tactless to rub in our awareness of the backwardness of others. But to compromise the content of rights to meet such needs and limitations is signally corrupting. Any general definition of a tolerable level of rights may actually place an undue burden on the least advanced peoples. But a minimal definition, made in the interests of the backward, too readily permits the more fortunate not only to rest on their oars, but even to recede from their best established practice without subjecting themselves to disapproval. It is therefore vital that an international bill of rights be at a minimum a statement of the best foreseeable achievement of the most advanced countries. Then indeed avoidance of insult to the more backward necessitates magnanimity. But the evils of condescending superiority are to be avoided by positive assistance based on recognition of equal commitment to such a bill under unequal conditions. Thereby we may combat a common enemy, consistent only in a rooted arbitrariness which glorifies statism, abuses power, and shows cavalier disrespect for persons.

America's interest in defense of the free world

Commitment by ourselves and by others to the principles of the open society, to the pursuit of the goal of personal self-realization, and to rights both as restrictions on power and as enabling means to well-being, give clues to the contours of foreign policy. Clear awareness of our moral purpose, grounded in our heritage, provides a basis for the separation and identification of sheep and goats, of friend and foe. By clarifying the nature of different expediencies, and their relation to principle, we can avoid confused realism and reap the reward of convinced allies possessed of high morale. By implementing the principles we profess, we can generate power beyond our own force by reason of purposes shared with others.

Once we have accepted the incompatibility and irreconcilability of polities based on respect for the person and tyrannies which deny a right to life, yet alone to the pursuit of happiness, our general policy becomes an aggressive defense against the latter. Our initial object is to contain them, to prevent their further expansion. Simultaneously we must seek to arouse and encourage opposition to them in their own countries. We must also strive to find and develop leadership and programs which offer a real alternative program suited to the people's needs and capable of winning their support and creating needful consensus. Then we must strive to overthrow the prevalent régimes. We must organize military might for their defeat should they themselves seek or force a showdown. We must promote the conditions for successful internal revolution with our moral and material aid. Any temporary peaceful intercourse with our opponents, and in particular any commerce between them and ourselves and our friends, becomes solely a matter of advantage for the moment, to be foregone at the point where theirs is the greater gain, materially or morally. Indeed, for the sake of principle and its clear proclamation to friends and enemies alike, it may be imperative to forego all economic intercourse, even at very high cost. Yet it is well not to be dogmatic on this point. Thus nonintercourse by Britain and some Continental countries with certain Russian satellites might severely harm the economy of the former, and on balance profit the Soviet régime. The duty to cut off one's material nose to improve one's moral face is not an unambiguously clear ethical dictate.

Apart from direct action against our enemies, our purpose is to win the tottering, the fearful, and the undecided by persuasion, by cautious aid, and by the promise of our way, and of support in our way. To that end, we must demonstrate to them that we have the will and the power to promote and protect in the world our own principle of life, and men's struggles under diverse and suitable institutions to pursue and achieve it. Further, we must recognize and support our true (as distinct from our temporary and nominal) allies who are committed to our generic values. We must do so even though by heritage, through lack of means, or by reason of limited experience and untried institutions, they do not subscribe fully to our theory nor follow our specific practice of the social nation. Through poverty and shortages or through past abuses, many peoples are forced towards a greater degree of statism, in the form of the socialist state, than we should regard as ideal. But our chief task is to protect and further the conditions of human dignity. We must combat the utopian chimera of tragedy eliminated, which is the death of personality. We must recognize those who share that cause, whatever their weaknesses. Even at high cost in sacrifice, we must give them all possible aid, comfort, and inspiration that they may strengthen their convictions, their institutions, and their efforts. We must prevent them from being disillusioned and feeling friendless. We must see to it that they do not succumb to the promise of shortcuts, to the hopes and fears of the desperate and the deluded, and to forceful power which at least professes a universal purpose and promotes it with missionary zeal.

A great nation, endowed with power and forced into leadership, can retain its position and secure its values only by making that power the servant of morality. Its appeal and its promise must be universal. Its authority in the world must be grounded in principled function serviceable to others as well as itself, rather than in protected privilege. In this sense, the American national interest is international. The values we hold are rooted in our institutions. But they enjoy vitality and security at home only insofar as they are goods for others. We must show that for them also such values are meaningful in principle and effectively realizable in practice, once given their own commitment and effort.

Foreign policy must first rest on a clarification of what we do espouse. Thereafter, it must be energetically conducted with a view to making our world view vital and appealing to others, as the common truths by which we and they live. That is the first and fundamental sharing; and happily, in the realm of final goods, the goods of mind and spirit, to share and disseminate is to increase and intensify, not to diminish and sacrificially forego. Next, it is necessary for us to support political institutions, governments, and public opinions which seem in intent and action most likely to further our grand design. We must combat, and aid others to combat, contrary viewpoints, parties, and practices. Likewise, we must promote, and ourselves adhere to and observe, an international system of rights based on the method of freedom. We must protect those rights against attack and abuse by avowed enemies of that method.

In the realm of more material and immediately practical aid, we must therefore organize our own defenses, and assist in the development and organization of those of other peoples and blocs, whether along the lines of NATO or by similar appropriate and acceptable techniques. On the bases of available resources and of potentials, we must give insurance of maximum available security against any attack, reasonably feared or possible, by the proclaimed enemies of gradualness and advocates of totalitarianism, under whatever rubric, and in the name of whatever ideal.

Such a policy must be designed to give full assurance to all peoples that there is a common cause of freedom. We must make clear that we regard it as in our interest, as well as theirs, to see freedom maintained everywhere by all means available. First of all, therefore, we must proclaim, publicly and convincingly, our abandonment of the idea that our sole concern is the defense of this country and its inhabitants or of the North American continent. Moreover, we must make it clear that our decision does not rest on a judgment of military feasibility, and would not be changed even were we completely sure that we could protect these shores by ourselves alone, and without bases outside them. Nor must we adopt a different policy simply because we deem that safety so acquired would not be lasting, though it is indeed probable that so exclusive a concern would in the long run leave us isolated, and might in due course lead to a concerted attack which, for all our resources, we could not lastingly withstand. A policy of exclusive defense, however practicable, would be erroneous because it would lead first to moral, and then to institutional, corruption at home. No immediate economies, no middle-run material gains, no temporary sense of security which comes from being uninvolved could offset that corruption.

The primary concern of the military man as expert is to protect the nation, conceived as population and resources organized within a territory. He makes his calculations on the basis of uses and losses of resources, of personnel and matériel. He assesses possible cost and partial sacrifices in relation to the security or survival of the whole. But the democratic public order of man the political animal has to be concerned with moral values, which it is its duty and interest to preserve and further. Here the military order is instrumental, as narrowly military calculations are materialist. Military considerations must be subordinate, not dominant and conclusive.

So to argue is not, manifestly, to proclaim the unimportance of defense of the territory, the people, and the developed resources of this country. Defense is a primary and proper concern of any nation. For a small nation, with limited resources and population, it may indeed be the sole consideration, because it may be the maximum potential. A nation fulfills its obligation by self-protection to the best of its ability. The interest of other similar nations in its defense is real, though limited. They are properly concerned that the political independence of its people be not forcefully terminated. Great allies are, however, especially interested in maximum self-help by such a nation, and the minimizing of need for military aid to it. In the case of a leading power such as these United States, however, the interest of others in its secure defense is far greater, simply because this country is in the widest sense what it was called in the last war: the arsenal of democracy. Insistence, therefore, that self-protection at home is alone not enough involves no denial of the fundamental duty of defense. It is predicated, rather, on the assumption that local defense is part of a total defense. We possess, and must allocate, resources for the whole task, even though those resources are not enough fully to meet all demands. We must do so under conditions where, because of the psychological and political consequences of a narrowly selfish defense, an emphasis on local American needs alone cannot lastingly achieve its own professed purpose. How much of our resources for defense should be concentrated on local protection, and how much should be committed to actual or potential military aid to others is in part, but only in part, a technical military and economic question.

The overall consideration is the need to defend against aggression all the freedom-loving peoples. It is necessary everywhere to prevent the forceful extension of control by the avowed enemies of life as a personal questing. The boundaries and the areas to be watched and defended are difficult to define with precision. The conditions of effective defense involve uncertain judgments. The ultimate costs are unpredictable. Yet the ramparts we watch and the frontiers we man are those of the whole free world. Even as strategy, that appeasement typified by Munich is doubtful defense indeed, all questions of morale and the need for positive principle apart. But, on the philosophy of democracy, of rights, and of personality here developed, it is utterly ruinous and corrupting. Our commitments can be limited only by our principles, which constitute our international interest, and by the limitation of our resources and those of our allies, which inevitably prohibit the ideal effectuation of those principles.

Effective defense of those principles involves, indeed, an expediential question. For this wealthy country, and indeed for the whole area and population to be defended, means are scarce when measured against the objective of perfect preparation to meet all possible aggressions, and to be equally able to do so now and at any future time. It is also necessary to maintain high standards of production and consumption at home, not simply for our own pleasure and comfort, but to combat propaganda against our system of political economy. It is likewise necessary, both for defense itself and for the effectiveness of the principles we support and share, to aid less developed countries towards improved living standards. Choices therefore have to be made; and even the most informed judgment in making them may in the end prove erroneous. But the acknowledged limitation of means and the inescapable uncertainties involved in actual choices, where there are many variables, are no warrant either for narrow and short-sighted selfishness or for a doctrine of specific and limited commitments based on the technical military judgment that these last may be perfectly met by means of calculable and limited assignment of manpower and matériel. With the means we have, we must do the best we can for the protection and material progress of the whole free world.

The proper implications are two. First, it is necessary for us and for those allied with us to be aware that circumstances may occur where their own resistance and our immediately available military aid may not be sufficient to prevent occupation nor to insure against heavy losses and destruction. Our first obligation is therefore not to create false illusions of security nor exaggerated views as to what we can and will do. There may be Dunkirks, or worse. But by the same token it is important to make clear that no ally who works for the common cause and places partial dependence on us will be treated as a means only. No people will be ruthlessly sacrificed either for temporary peace or on purely strategic considerations. We must never forget that other peoples are also composed of persons and collectively possess the culture and aspirations of human societies not less than we ourselves. Our commitment where such peoples have to be sacrificed temporarily or partially as means to a common end in which they also share must be a national restatement of General MacArthur's celebrated "I shall return." For the freedom of every people from an alien and imposed domination is a condition of that collective security which is our own interest and ideal.

Secondly, however, decisions as to what are appropriate contributions to a common defense, what are the obligations of the parties, and also under what conditions any particular member may have to be temporarily and partially sacrificed for a common good, necessitate collective consultation and the consent of the participating members. The reaching of such decisions, as well as subsequent planning to put them into effect, are among the central purposes of United Nations itself, of NATO-type organizations, and of hemispheric or continental political and economic unions. Such organizations are also the appropriate organs for judging whether their members, on the basis of assessed capacity and of their own consent, have carried out their obligations towards their own and the collective defense; and for bringing pressure on them to remedy failures in duty to the common cause. Likewise, they can give moral sanction to any lessening of our commitment to support nations which do not do their part, though expediency and the overall interests of our bloc may dictate support even of those links in our chain which are weak through their own fault.

Issues as to the amount and nature of our defenses and the total defense effort will still remain. For to state that our military policy must be conceived and shaped in the collective interest of the bloc we lead does not itself solve questions as to long- and short-term balancings in defense measures. Assessment of the relative importance of our own security as center and leader and the needs and claims of allies closer to an actual or potential firing line is a thorny question, in the absence of an impartial judge. Internally, too, we have to decide on the proper balance between peacetime industry, normal consumption, desirable investment, and enjoyment of leisure, on the one hand, and the urgencies of immediate defense and lasting preparedness, on the other. Moreover, every component unit of this collective order which comprises the free world must necessarily retain a primary responsibility for its own internal choices as to development and use of resources and the use of human energies. Certainly we ourselves would insist, and do insist, that decisions on such matters which primarily affect us are ours to make, and ours alone. What is more, we quite properly insist that it would grievously harm us without helping others if we were to ruin our economy, destroy our material welfare, and sacrifice our future development in an attempt to meet fully all the economic and military needs of all present or future allies, whether those needs are measured by their present distance from our own standards and accomplishments or by some lesser criterion of adequacy based on the achievements of Western industrial society.

The engagement in which we are involved and the very purpose we embody and serve imply a long struggle and a total overall commitment, of which even so-called total war would itself be only a part. We are the leaders of one side and one philosophy, which we hold universal and true. We are engaged in a total struggle of ways of life, of looking at life, and of conducting life in society. The rightness of our values does not depend on success. But their maintenance and institutional realization do. Yet, insofar as the conditions of struggle permit, it is necessary for us to avoid the frantic abandonment of lasting goods. We must resist forebodings of crisis and impending doom. Otherwise we lose the chance to demonstrate to others the superiority of our way through our own continuous achievement of better living standards and greater human satisfaction. It is no less necessary to make needful sacrifices and adequate provision for defense against forceful attacks in order that the very opportunity for future development and for the triumph of those views be not destroyed. For protection against our totalitarian opponent both we and our allies must have sufficient guns. But for triumph in ideological warfare we need to show that we can enjoy both guns and butter and that we can help our allies to enjoy more bread without risking their safety and independence.

But to achieve our ends we have variously to persuade others, to listen to their opinions, and to accommodate ourselves to their needs and feelings. We must use existing common institutions to reach recommendations, judgments, and decisions. By such means the calculations and plans made are apt to be well-informed and are most likely to achieve general acceptance and be supported by co-operation in carrying them out. Such methods help us to avoid the actual limitations of selfish and short-sighted bias, as well as the accusation that we are acting from prejudicial interest. Under the aegis of a shared ideal, we can escape utopian delusions. At the same time, our recognition of the nature and needs of the common enterprise and of its relation to our own lasting interest constitutes an effective basis for responsibility in determining issues of security and welfare at home as against abroad, and for assessing and weighing long- and short-term considerations. Errors may still be made, since biases are inescapable. The espousal of an American concept of international interest, and the acceptance of international institutions as vehicles for forwarding that interest as a common cause and for critical limiting of unilateral action, are no sure guarantees of success. Fortune still plays its part in human affairs, and peoples need the nerve of failure. But such a policy and attitude is most calculated to utilize the instrumental means of wealth and force effectively. For by reason of moral purpose and appeal it engenders and harnesses power. It overcomes American weaknesses due to lack of sympathy, or positive suspicion, by others. It prevents that guilty sense of inner corruption on our part which can arise either from selfish isolation or from self-seeking nationalistic imperialism.

International economic policy for America

Defense itself is part of a total struggle of social orders. It is, therefore, only one element in the overall development and flourishing of our own type of political society. That type is the sole consistent way to sustained fulfillment of persons. Its well-being as an instrumental order devoted to a moral and spiritual purpose shared by others is the initial basis of its power. Policy is the means to create such power through the propagating and implementing of the informing principle. Diplomacy and strategy are subordinate instrumentalities. They are directed by policy. They inform the policy-maker of the conditions of his task, of the means available to him, and of presently limiting factors. But the policy-maker must be aware that internal and international politics are inescapably one, and he must act accordingly. They are interdependent parts of that American adventure which is lastingly committed to the realism of idealism by very reason of the moral aspiration which is the dynamo of our institutional life.

The political commitments resultant on such purpose, and in particular the consequences of the basic concepts of rights, have already been clarified. The contours of such policy have been further indicated by discussion of defense. The implications for economic policy in the international realm are likewise readily discernible. The economic order is a fundamental instrumentality of the good life. Its healthy functioning is a vital buttress to that constitutionalism which protects and furthers the pursuit of that life. The development and blessings of industrialism are the matrix of effective constitutional democracy, which is the political method of freedom for personality.

At home or abroad, we cannot effectively further the interests of our social order, which are ultimately moral concern for persons, either by an irresponsible economic individualism or by a statism which glorifies power and represses creative energies. At home it is necessary to develop the public-welfare society. That society rests on co-partnership between government and the institutions of the economic order. Its objectives are effective predictability and the elimination of fruitless wastes. Its ends are maximum service and provision of material means for the pursuit of the good life by very diverse personalities. Abroad, we need to sponsor analogous practices and to further like ends. The venturings of merely selfish economic individualists are not today possible as the central directives and instruments of our international economic policy, by reason of the policies of other governments. That difficulty apart, reliance on such a technique would mean our lack of effective control of our own policy. We would thus be unable freely to promote and further interests shared by ourselves and our allies. We would also be subject to unintended public commitments as a result of such private venturings.

On the other hand, statism, whether its form be centralized planning, overextended bureaucratic controls, or state socialism, means a needless denial of variety at home. It results in loss of experimentation. It leads to frustration of persons in their search for satisfaction through calling and enterprise. Finally, quite apart from its indirect threats to democratic freedom, it produces a rigidifying of the economic structure and a diminution or cessation of economic progress. In the area of international economic relations, such statism leads first to autarky, the equivalent in economics of isolationism in politics and exclusive local defense in military affairs. It leads thereafter to an economic imperialism which is the complement in ethos and effect of a political policy of the search for power over others by force or intimidation.

The United States has, then, to devise international economic policies which depart from the old dogma of international free trade as complement of an international political order of co-operation, as propounded by Woodrow Wilson. We must resist the temptation to seek self-sufficiency, politically delusive even if technically feasible. Yet we can find no solution through the insights of the late Charles A. Beard. He saw the inadequacy of both the preceding solutions; but he himself offered a third choice designed to serve an exclusive national interest. Beard correctly perceived that the chance actions of private enterprisers abroad led to unpredictables for the statesman. Unpredictable private decisions were incompatible with any coherent public-welfare policy at home. They produced changes in power relations between ourselves and others which were accidental, uncontrolled, and normally without clear political intent. They made the formulation and execution of a coherent international economic policy almost impossible. Yet Beard realized that the needs of an industrial civilization made trade with others imperative. The earlier solution of Fichte's *The Closed Trade State* was simply not available in the present-day world, if, indeed, it had ever been. It was necessary, therefore, to control the activities of

American business engaged in foreign trade first to secure stable well-being at home, and then to prevent the growth of industries abroad in a way detrimental to our own national interest, conceived as sustained differential welfare and power. It was, above all, needful to insure that changes in the power of others in relation to ourselves should not be at the mercy of private acts which were not related to public policy or designed with conscious reference to national interest.

The Beard position revealed profound insights. It was critically sound. It rested on its author's long-lived recognition of the interdependence of economics and politics; on his awareness of the primacy of statesmanship in ultimately compounding interests; and on his perception that policy must be an overall and total thing, without artificial dichotomy between internal and international affairs. Beard was emphatic that free enterprise as free venturing and free trade was a hopeless impediment to effective foreign policy, once one accepted the fact of American power and participation in the international order. It meant weakness and uncertainty on our part where others were clear and certain. At the same time the very nature of our industrial technology, its raw material needs, and the scale of our productive capacity made isolationism as autarky, even at its best and most successful, a needless privation of wealth and a self-imposed and uncompensated limitation on national power. A controlled and directed pursuit of national self-interest in an international political economy was the only sensible solution.

The elimination of political irresponsibility promised by such a design was no doubt a real benefit to be derived from Beard's prescription. So, too, was the overcoming of the cross-purposes of private interests, which would be duly assessed and judged in the light of long-term stability in the internal economy. But from an international viewpoint, the Beard solution was unsatisfactory and politically dangerous. In the existing conduct of international economic affairs under the law of comparative advantage there was already a hidden inequity. For the operation of that law subtly imposed the lasting disadvantage of resigned acceptance of inequality between particular nations as the sole road to betterment by means of exchanges which were on those terms mutually profitable. Beard offered a different inequity, which arose out of the frank compulsive pressure of the stronger political economy and its interests as the condition for trade and development by others. In many cases, other peoples would be still more clearly confined to colonialism and would be lastingly purveyors of raw materials. For we would deny them opportunity for potential industrial development through refusal of capital and capital goods, should it be in our political and economic interest to do so. We would assume that nations were in political-economic competition. Our purpose would be lastingly to enjoy, and, if possible to increase, our differentially high standards of living and of power. Neither imperialist nor isolationist, Beard's program was one of insulationism through participation in international affairs on the basis of power politics and power economics.

For all its coherence, such a proposed policy is less than adequate to deal with the issues of a world where two professed sets of values— and ways to attain those values—are in deadly conflict. Indeed, it has already proved inadequate to cope with the conflict between the democratic order and Nazism, despite the avowed particularism of the latter. Beard's very sound insight that our whole way of life and of getting a living is involved in international economic relations, and that national affairs and international relations constitute a continuum, has been rendered abortive by the attempt to make policy the handmaid of a purely American interest, unilaterally defined. The United States can achieve lasting well-being only by demonstration of its embodiment of a moral code of universal appeal. Other peoples must be convinced that America's leadership in the industrial order and its consequent enjoyment of superior standards of living give promise of amelioration in their lot. They must further be convinced that it is our intention to promote their sharing in the betterment which an industrial order makes possible. We must demonstrate that we can bring to them the blessings and give them the strength of the industrial order. We must make clear that, in following us, they will not have to sacrifice the values of humanity fruitlessly. Rather, they will gain through continuous realization of those values. Only by following such policies and bringing about such conviction in others can the United States hope to protect its material interests and to preserve effectively the rational values in its tradition, which alone constitute its inner dynamics and its basic claim to be a world leader.

The problems involved in accomplishment of that purpose necessitate the same sort of calculations and balancings as those already analyzed in discussing defense. Indeed, military defense is in reality a subordinate area of the total pattern of a political economy devised and directed by realistic idealism. For the immense proportions of bipolar conflict involve the creation, the husbanding, and the use of power on behalf of our system of values. Any more limited interpretation is the road to serfdom, first by self-betrayal, and at last by inadequacy of power and consequent defeat.

With our assistance and by the use of their own energies, depressed and devastated countries in Europe and backward and overpopulated countries in the Far East and elsewhere may achieve the blessings of industrial and modern agricultural development. In the process, they may avoid the drawbacks of totalitarian rule. They may progressively realize the values of free persons under liberating institutions. Nevertheless, in the realm of overt material and organizational accomplishment, the imposed and planned totalitarian order enjoys an initial advantage. Through discipline and by means of training without education, communism after the Soviet pattern provides a short-cut by which to attain the outward visible signs of a modern economy without regard to the inward spiritual grace of the democratic industrial order. Its immediate price is, indeed, the foregoing of present enjoyment of adequate consumer goods. But by means of delusive promises for the future, it can often persuade men that the price has to be paid and is worth paying. On occasion its propaganda actually evokes initial enthusiasm for such sacrifice by exploiting men's concern for their children, and their children's children. Our difficult task is to persuade others that such sacrifice is vain, and that the appeal to them to make it is a vicious exploitation of their decent impulses and noble concerns. We must make them see that a progressive but imperfect realization at once of economic modernization and of personal freedom is both continuously and lastingly more rewarding than conspicuously rapid material advance in the creation of capital goods at the price of spiritual death or perversion.

The actual failure of so-called communism to provide a high standard of living here-now may prove helpful in this endeavor. But we must remember that past privations suffered by agrarian peoples limit legitimate expectations, and we must not exaggerate the degree of immediate betterment that they may anticipate from following our design. Malnutrition, illiteracy, and absence of skills can be remedied only with time and effort. But those who suffer these ills, like the deprived everywhere, are apt to seek shortcuts. Their very lack of training renders them unaware of the ultimate price, as their present condition may cause them radically to discount the future. In the competition for men's hearts and minds, the unscrupulous peddlers of panaceas generally enjoy an advantage over the more sober and conscientious propagandist. Here, as in so many other places, a social Gresham's Law holds true: the bad money tends to drive out the good. As we are aware, it is not easy to persuade a prosperous people to actual sacrifices. It is still harder for those most prosperous to persuade a deprived people who envy and want to share their prosperity that they can do so only by going slow and by sacrificing what our bitterest enemies assure them that they can have at once, and that we viciously withhold. Our task is to demonstrate both that the Communist way is inherently unlikely to bring the anticipated and promised result and that our way, without demand for total present sacrifices of liberty, is actually the route to sure future attainment of material well-being and of personal fulfillments. We must convince them that it is the best way by very reason of its values and of our genuine determination to aid in their realization.

Such a demonstration requires our unstinting and intelligent aid to promote and further self-help elsewhere, without regard to economic returns, to profit and loss. Bookkeeping considerations, a search for favorable balances, and the desire to preserve our differential advantages are either irrelevant or antagonistic to that moral purpose which is our long-term interest and the genesis by right use of lasting power. In the past, indeed, we have shown ourselves to be a generous people wherever disaster has struck. We have used both private and governmental agencies to bring immediate relief, to rebuild shattered cities and shattered lives. In the process, we have revealed to the full our organizing genius and our capacity for getting things done. More recently, too, by both public and private means we have given sustained help to peoples and persons who have suffered the devastation of war and the physical and spiritual impoverishment of long occupation or longer tyranny. Wherever we have been givers pure and simple, and the suffering and urgency were obvious, our record has been superb. But where others' needs are long-term reconstruction or development, we have tended both to apply other criteria than need and mutual aid and to become confusedly critical. We have then noted that charity has not always begotten gratitude and has sometimes led to dependency and to demands as of right. We have failed to be sufficiently aware of others' difficulties in being gracious and balanced recipients, especially where poverty is grim and not temporary. We have not fully allowed for the complex interplay of pride and of lost dignity; of guilt and assertive self-righteousness; of calculatingness and a frustrated yearning for effective self-help. Nor have we been clearly aware that ingratitude can follow from hopes initially created by our generosity, and we are then disappointed when we switch back to hard-boiled calculatingness and considerations of our own advantage.

Despite our commitment to the Point Four program and to the Marshall Plan, congressional and public debate and the critical attitude of large parts of the business community have all revealed rather widespread fear that we might dissipate our resources and deprive ourselves in a futile subsidization of Europe and Asia. The critics have felt that we could not expect proportionate economic returns and could not surely count on any sure political advantage from such a course.

Such judgments have not been entirely without warrant. In comparison with America, the average living standards of the Far East are abysmally low. Population pressure is enormous, the normal life expectancy short. Nor is there any certainty that, in the short run, industrialization and resources development would alleviate, rather than increase, the miseries of the masses, and that it would bring about a decline in net population growth. At the same time, the lack of full literacy—not to mention general and technical education in our own sense—makes Western democracy an improbable immediate adventure in most Eastern countries. The spreading there of aspirations to national dignity is indeed among the conspicuous events of our time. Hardly less impressive is the growing unwillingness to accept any governments, domestic or foreign, which manifestly function in the interests of a limited and privileged group. To be successful, Eastern governments must now institute, or at least sponsor, reforms actually or professedly on behalf of the masses. They must provide opportunities for new men to develop and use talents and to rise in position and power. Nevertheless the very conditions of Oriental society and its past heritage make the rapid and full adoption of democratic institutions and the practice of popular participation in politics unlikely, even impractical, because they are immediately unworkable. As a consequence, we ourselves are tempted to look on economic aid to Eastern countries which goes beyond our own immediate and expedient interest as futile and wasteful. We likewise question the value of attempts there to support and further a political life positively consonant with our own political philosophy. Our attitude does not rest on ill will or indifference, but on a feeling of futility and impotence.

The economic problem of Western Europe also involves population pressures. But the context is radically different. Europe is suffering from depleted economic resources and from inadequate or inadequately reconstructed industrial equipment, despite vast strides in reconstruction or new development in some European countries. In many cases, it has not learned how to limit effectively the power of privileged groups, who, as heirs or assigns of ancient hierarchical society, continue to enjoy disproportionate consideration, and thereby generate Marxist convictions within the masses. Our own awareness of this situation is one cause of our hesitancy to give adequate economic aid. For by so doing we might also give ultimate aid and comfort to our avowed opponents. Alternatively, we might encourage socialist and statist undertakings not consonant with our own philosophy. We feel it may in the long run prove wiser simply to buttress those forces clearly antagonistic to our Soviet enemies by limited and expedient aid.

We are tempted to ignore the fact that such groups may be unpopular in their own countries and that their undemocratic ways may reflect on us and alienate rank and file support for our cause.

In short, those who advocate a protection and husbanding of our own resources, and a limited and calculating use of them to succor others where they may serve our interests, argue one of two things. Either they maintain that an attempt to raise standards generally throughout the world is hopeless, within any foreseeable future, and can only ruin ourselves by leveling our standards downward; or they are convinced that in the rest of the world American political and social institutions are unappreciated and will not be emulated. On both grounds, narrow and immediate considerations of purely American power and prosperity should govern policy, since they alone lead to sanely useful activities. Such critics of more generous aid to others do not deny the uniqueness of the American experience and achievement. They rejoice in the American combination of industrialism and democracy. They stress the values of our pluralist social nation devoted to the well-being of persons. They simply insist that our way of life is either unwanted or impossible of achievement elsewhere. Under such circumstances, our national interest and our first duty is to preserve and further that way at home. Thus we may insure the welfare of our own citizens, set an example to the world, and make our maximum contribution to human culture.

On the other hand, if we make the salvation and welfare of others our prime concern, we shall sacrifice a great and dynamic social order to a naïve humanitarianism. We all know that to distribute income equally to all persons within our own society would profit the poor little, and not lastingly. Yet it would deprive us of investment capital and of that spending which promotes culture. Likewise, thoroughgoing economic assistance to other peoples would in due course ruin our industrial society by killing technological progress. It would lower our living standards without lasting gain to the world at large.

The case is an impressive one. A realistic assessment of economic, social, and political conditions elsewhere, particularly in the Orient, permits no easy optimism as to the ease or speed of achievement of anything approximating our own level of income, of leisure, and of opportunity for diverse personal fulfillments. Nevertheless, the policies advocated or implied are themselves, on any but the shortest view, unrealistic. Likewise they are lacking in idealism. For our insights and achievements rest on principles of universal applicability. They hold promise for all and must be available for export, even though we ourselves are, and seek to remain, their first beneficiaries.

Even on a purely realistic calculation, their export is the price of success in our struggle with a régime which proffers to people outside its immediate orbit a method and organization for achieving rapid modernization and industrialization, widespread economic well-being, and a general participation in the processes and the rewards of social transformation. The Soviet leadership offers agrarian nations technical aid and training, material aid, markets, and political support in their undertakings if they will agree to follow its pattern, accept its dogma, and submit to its primacy and control. The questions of Soviet sincerity, and of the appropriateness of its means to others' ends, are irrelevant while sacrifice rests on hope and while tyranny masquerades as a noble struggle for creative transformation and for its necessary condition. Before we can press such questions with a reasonable chance of attention we must offer a persuasive alternative. We must show that we follow up our ethical professions with practical assistance and that our statements of common interests do not mean simply that others should behave in ways that suit us, while we remain undisturbed by their wishes and unburdened by their needs.

Before the Second World War the Japanese had themselves developed a doctrine from which we might today profit. Their concept of a Co-Prosperity Sphere in Asia was conceived as a useful technique for gaining Eastern support in their struggle with the West. It offered to Asiatic peoples the hope of progress without reliance either on Western Capitalism or on Soviet Communism. The Japanese propaganda was a technique for achieving domination in Asia. The leadership and ambitions of the military undermined any chance that the Co-Prosperity professions might become practice. But the teaching itself emphasized the distance between Western democratic professions and our professed concern for the freedom and well-being of Oriental peoples on the one hand and our seemingly self-interested practice, which aimed at profit, privilege, and power. It noted that our equating of democracy with freedom for Western enterprisers was scarcely compatible with the material and political development of Eastern peoples. Our system provided no answer to their problems, since it contained no program by which they could modernize their economies to their own profit. Our individual enterprise would give us the lion's share; while a native individualistic capitalism would not be able to create rapid industrialization and would not profit the whole society. By contrast, the concept of a Co-Prosperity Sphere professed to be one of planned development jointly by Japan and its less advanced allies, with mutual gains based on shared responsibilities and common efforts. It involved a modification and extension of Japan's own Zaibatsu system, wherein economic cartels were intimately related to government in a collectivist capitalism which was also an Oriental national socialism. Political and economic institutions co-operated, and indeed fused. Our own cult of littleness and opposition to trusts was avoided. So was the irresponsible corporation, the state within a state. And so was communism, with its dogmatic totalitarianism.

Individualism after the pattern of early industrialism offers no hope of rapid industrialization to backward or agrarian countries, especially since they often lack the spread of scientific knowledge, the political experience, and the risk capital already available in England at the Industrial Revolution. Nor are such countries ready to accept a doctrine of democratic capitalism which at once leaves them to harsh and fruitless struggles and permits profitable investment and control by our own advanced corporate industry and commerce. Our advocacy of such courses appears as lack of interest in their welfare and exclusive concern with our own advantage. Our failure to offer a workable alternative is a surrender by default to Communism. Our only hope and our real obligation is to develop our own version of a Co-Prosperity Sphere, without the drawbacks and the hypocrisy which marked the Japanese version. The solution must be applicable wherever needed within the democratic bloc. It must avoid the sinister antidemocratic and exploitative orientation which was one element in Japan's own Zaibatsu system. It must apply in the international sphere, and for the beneficial development of industrially backward countries, our own best practice of co-operative interaction between business and government for the benefit of the social nation.

Such an undertaking is possible by means of a more thorough-going and integrated development of the Point Four program in conjunction with international financial assistance given under the auspices of the International Bank and of the International Monetary Fund respectively. Its effectuation would not only make possible our effective economic aid to present allies in the West without a distracting and disturbing emphasis on economic individualism. It would also permit the whole democratic bloc, with American leadership, to muster its resources so as to offer a genuine alternative to Communism in China and the Far East and to Russia's East European satellites. It would aid in the spreading of disaffection behind the Iron and Silken Curtains by giving hope of material betterment with and through freedom, and by spreading conviction that we understood the needs, and sympathized practically with the aspirations, of peoples far different in heritage and situation from ourselves. For such a co-prosperity program would be genuine. It would embrace and implement the Japanese promise of common sharing in progressive material development. Aside from practicality, such a teaching would have moral appeal, something not true of either the dogma of economic individualism or the doctrine of our own immediate economic national interest as a criterion for trade and investment.

Achievements and prospects

Despite our recent tendency towards intransigent and narrowed dogmatism in determining conditions for collaboration with our allies, we have avoided both utopian idealism and nationalistic realism alike in

the conduct of World War II and in our postwar diplomacy and foreign policy. We have shown reasonable awareness of time and human
imperfection as limits on possible achievement. Despite naïveté about
the U.S.S.R., despite initial misinformation as to the nature of Communism in China, and despite internal appeasements of both reactionary
and radical extremists, we have also shown our capacity to adapt to the
conditions of the present world and to pursue generally enlightened
policies in it. From Bretton Woods and Dumbarton Oaks to leadership
of the United Nations in the Korean international law enforcement
action, our policy, aided by well-directed criticism and by resultant
correction of lapses, has with considerable consistency been on the side
of using and strengthening international organization and international
economic co-operation. Where we have failed, we have done so at least
as often by reason of lack of imagination and daring due to the pressure
of ungenerous concepts of national interest as from unrealistic confidence and misplaced trust.

At root our policy has embodied a hesitant and imperfect recognition that the interests of the United States are international and
collective, not nationalistic and exclusive. It has revealed a consonance
between the American antistatist tradition of freedom and statesmanship on behalf of the social nation and the aspirations of other peoples.
It has supported their endeavors to escape from economic want and to
attain political security. It has demonstrated that today a realistic concept of national interest must be based in theory and practice on the
genuine morality of respect for the finite particularity of peoples. It
has rested on a perception that all peoples share a common humanity. It
has recognized that, in a transition stage from old nationalism to new
world order, they strive uncertainly, tentatively, adaptively, and yet
determinedly to create institutions and mechanisms for the furtherance of that humanity without abandonment of cherished diversities.
However uncertainly, we have proclaimed that in such a world the
United States must interpret its national interest as international interest. For we are heirs to Western culture. In the past, we were creators
of new patterns for the more effective realization of ancient human insights. Today we are possessors of power for leadership. Rights and

duties follow, in a situation where practical success and moral obligation are luckily consonant and interdependent.

Whatever the difficulties and the dangers of our present position, the future does not look unpromising. True, some sections of the business community, recently eager to decrease the range, the costs, and the inhibiting effect of government controls over their enterprises, may also strive to maximize individual business enterprise and minimize governmental aid abroad. Such a course would clearly make coherent and sustained policy difficult. It would involve a failure to subordinate private economics to public politics. It would decrease our appeal and effectiveness in the world by emphasizing our calculating self-interest.

Nevertheless, isolationist sentiment itself appears to be recessive as a business attitude. Indeed, large portions of the business community appear to be aware of their public responsibility. They perceive that it is not enough to confine themselves to their private tasks. They are aware that it is unwise to confine government to support of their enterprises, or to nonintervention in their conduct. Indeed, many business leaders have shown a willingness to participate in government and to give those officially responsible for its conduct the benefit of their advice. They have done so, often at considerable cost to themselves, from a consciousness of public obligation, rather than as a matter of self-protection or self-seeking alone. They have asked only for a régime in which they can participate and be consulted as respectable and respected citizens, and a public attitude not weighted by the assumption that they are in their normal behavior actual or potential public enemies. There seems a real likelihood that many leaders in our economy will become partners in that co-organic public welfare state which is the necessity of our time and place. They are prepared to regard government as useful instrumentality rather than dangerous enemy. Provided they do not totally disappoint expectations, our unique achievement of the public welfare society seems secure.

Their participation may also be expected to emphasize the necessities of coherence in foreign policy. They will come to perceive the necessary limits of private enterprise in international affairs, and the need to subordinate private ambitions for economic gain in order to avoid those self-contradictory consequences from the viewpoint of the nation which Beard long since described. They will come to realize that economic instrumentalities may and should be used to give us lasting leadership through ideological and moral appeal, rather than as means to achieve temporary ascendancy through superior compulsive power. Indeed, once they grasp the basic nature of bipolar conflict as a struggle for leadership in industrializing the nonindustrial world, in creating mass markets and higher living standards, and in promoting leisure for consumption, our manufacturing and business leaders may accept the imaginative challenge to their creative organizing ability. Eager to exercise their peculiar craftsmanship and to enjoy power attained by means of efficient performance of their function, they may subordinate narrow and partially unreal considerations of profit to the statesmanlike task of promoting American triumph through our leadership in fulfilling the world's demands. Thereby, and thereby alone, can the errors and evils of Soviet Communism be combatted. Thereby Western leadership can be assured. Thereby we may in due time achieve the means to the triumphant realization, in a world-wide society of societies, of man the ultimate person.

Meanwhile, whatever the injustices of recent criticism of our foreign policy and however unwarranted the extreme lack of confidence in its conduct, support of the present administration rests, among other things, on a conviction of its knowledge and competence in foreign affairs and of its understanding of the nature and needs of bipolar conflict. Moreover, though only yesterday popular aspiration seemed to be towards disengagement in Korea, and perhaps towards a general withdrawal from global commitments, the underlying need was for positive confidence which could overcome uncertainty and negative fear. That need has already been satisfied in large measure, without fundamental changes in policy, even though the peace which men hoped would follow an armistice seems still far distant. But our final success in Korea taught us a lesson: far from insisting on any withdrawal or compromise in our dealings with the Soviet bloc, the American people endorsed an aggressive and forthright policy, despite a minority's desire to withdraw from U.N. and world commitments. They did so, moreover, with a clear awareness of possible costs. (The later settlement did so prevail, even though the results reached involved a compromise and revealed a moderation which led some falsely to infer an abandonment of firmness.) Such confidence in executive leadership, provided it is maintained, should of itself facilitate the task of congressmen in instructing and leading their electorates. They may find themselves delivered from the need to reflect, even when they do not embody or encourage, popular fears and withdrawals. They may be enabled effectively to discourage any future clamor for an immediate safety and, if conflict occurs, an appeasing peace, where the consequences would be disastrous.

Such public confidence as we now possess creates the needful aggressive commitment to our moral tradition and purpose. It overcomes escapism. It avoids the merely artificial unity of dogmatic bipartisanship. It helps beget that conscious consensus on fundamentals so requisite to the health of our ideas and institutions at home, and to their successful championing and spread in the world. Our exaggerated fearfulness of real, but limited, threats of subversion at home and our unconfident resistance to the Soviet pattern and progress abroad have together constituted our recent weakness in the midst of strength. They have hidden from us, not less than from others, the superior progressiveness and promise of our own lasting way. And, while no combination of right and power guarantees success in the world, their joint organization as a positive crusade based on universal appeal is our own and the world's best hope. For power is generated by shared purpose. The idealism of such sharing is the most realistic, and the sole permanently rewarding, realism.

VII

American policy and citizen participation

The means and ends of our policy

To gain an effective foreign policy, we Americans must adopt our own theory and practice of constitutional democracy to fit the very different social and cultural traditions of other peoples. We must place our emphasis on the trend and potentiality of their institutional systems rather than on their instant achievement. We must be fully aware that in many countries limited literacy and political inexperience make the immediate realization of our way of life manifestly impossible. But we must never lose sight of the essential values embodied in our system. We must sell them to others. We must see to it that others do not sell them short. For our concern for personality and our stress on means and ends as both continuous and concomitant constitute the basis of an aggressive reply to the Communist profession and promise. They are the very ground for confidence in the superiority of our case. They enable us to avoid a defensiveness which is at once apologetic and glaringly self-interested.

Yet, even given our commitment to the principle and our positive good will to follow it in practice, the difficulties of practical implementation are great. Past experience with China is here illuminating. The widespread and long-lived belief that the Chinese Communists were well-intentioned agrarians, even if not totally unwarranted at the start, soon distorted sound calculations as to a possible basis for a progressive Chinese régime based on co-operation. Later, we too readily gave support to Chiang Kai-Shek as the enemy of our Japanese enemies without sufficient control of our aid. We failed to insist that the condition of aid must be reform to secure a lasting, stable, more broadly based, and popularly appealing régime. That failure rested initially on a forgetting of principle. It rested finally on a false calculation of power, of which party needed the other most: our very eagerness first to contain, and then to defeat, Japan permitted the Generalissimo to out-bluff us. Yet our failure also resulted from the difficulty of finding an effective third force. Such a force had to be non-Communist. It had to be progressive, reformist, and uncorrupt. It had to possess sufficient appeal to be made genuinely powerful by our aid and sufficient prestige to warrant our insistence on its inclusion in government as a major partner. It did not exist. It still needs to be created. Our lasting problem in China, even given eventual Communist defeat, will be how to promote its creation. For it is clear that only a despairing disillusion with Communism could lead to effective recapture of that country by the Nationalist government, however great our material and military support of its program for reconquest of Chinese territory. It is no less clear that a stable government of that vast land would be lastingly unlikely on the present narrow base. No American policy confined to support of such leadership can win or hold the enthusiasm and support of other Asiatic peoples or overcome the anti-Western orientation of a revolutionary nationalism.

The lack of a third force still marks many countries or areas of Asia. It is genuinely difficult for us at once to support unpopular anti-Communist groups on grounds of immediate urgency and to encourage and help to create the requisite parties and leadership which can lastingly and convincingly proffer an acceptable path to modernization.

For the condition of their acceptance is commitment to a seeking after social justice. They must promote the general welfare consonantly with observance of the overall method of freedom. Their aim must be progress towards democracy, of which the first prerequisites are popular education and raised living standards.

Our task today is to encourage and develop the necessary leadership. In giving economic aid, we must always insist on its proper use for the good of the intended beneficiaries. We must devise effective sanctions to prevent abuse or misuse. Where possible, we must utilize the United Nations and its international financial institutions as the most appropriate instrument whereby to create a shared interest in imperative undertakings and the needed sanctions. For we must avoid the stigma of unwarranted and self-interested interference and intervention.

While the situation in Europe is radically different, the need to give sustained economic assistance in such a way as to strengthen democratic forces is equally real. There, too, it is imperative to insist that moneys and goods which we provide be used for the intended purposes, and to the advantage of the intended beneficiaries. In Western Europe, moreover, we are even less justified in supporting those who seek to regain or to establish privileged position. For industry is well developed, political consciousness has long since awakened, and participation by the rank and file in public life is a cherished right. It is not necessary for us to rely on a very limited group which is not democratic in viewpoint as the only effective leadership against Communism and the only alternative to it. The past ascendancy of such groups has been a major cause of indignation and lack of public morale. Their existence and their actions have encouraged the workers to support Communism. Today, any buttressing we give to such groups plays still more into Communist hands. For when such groups misuse or misappropriate aid which we provide for reconstruction, anti-American sentiment is strengthened. This country must not appear to dictate to European peoples who are rendered sensitive by suffering and by declining power. But for us to permit misuse of assistance for the profit of limited groups, and without general benefits, is in the eyes of the rank and file precisely illegitimate intervention, even though it involves no positive action. On the other hand, a proper watchfulness on our part and an efficient control to insure gains in general welfare from American or international assistance would be fully acceptable. It would appear as proper support of a broadly based drive to achieve at once effective production and general benefits from renewed energies.

Our need in Europe is to recognize that *les classes dirigeantes* (the leaders in industry and finance who seemingly correspond to our own manufacturing and business classes) in general do not possess the attitude and outlook of our own captains and managers of industry. They do not possess the same prestige. They do not respond to the same motivations. They do not share the same attitudes. They do not pursue the same objectives. They do not hold the same view of the purpose of politics. Likewise, European social-welfare politics with its socialist programs results in large part from the failures in social responsibility of a major segment of the investing and industrial leadership groups. It is also a consequence of poverty in resources and of relative decline in economic position of that region. The American indictment of the evils of statism is indeed correct. For the end product of statism is totalitarianism and the total denial of personal freedom. Even before that stage is reached, men's energies are inhibited rather than released. Nevertheless, it is our interest and obligation to perceive the current practical and moral need in many nations of Europe for a large degree of state action and control, and for a far more thorough-going program of social welfare, including a good deal of socialism, than is requisite or tolerable under our more favorable conditions. For there a socialistic political economy is the sole effective insurance against Communism. The only other choice would be a fascist totalitarianism, which we would deplore as much as Communism. Happily, such régimes would in several major countries be neither stable nor popular.

We must be the chief financiers and the primary source of technical and expert personnel and of an economic and technical assistance program, whether carried out by ourselves directly or through United Nations institutions. The purpose of such a program is to develop local resources and skills in all areas not under Communist control. In the process, social dislocations must be minimized. The local inhabitants must strive for self-dependence under self-direction. If they are to do so, they must look forward to enjoyment in due course of the standards of living, of welfare, and of leisure necessary to free men. It is our vital interest to demonstrate the possibility of such achievement and to assist them in making it reality. Thereby we may prove that Communism under Russian auspices, or on any totalitarian pattern, is neither necessary *to* achievement nor superior *in* achievement. Rather, it needlessly demands sacrifices of liberty. Through its means it pointlessly perverts its professed moral ends and fails to attain them.

The human lot is, we repeat, inescapably tragic. Irony is deeply embedded in history. Tensions in and between societies are inescapable. The Communist analysis of the causes of such human ills is superficial. Its solution is utopian. Its practice brings greater and needless evils. By contrast, the Western ethic accepts the inescapable limits of our lot, but strives to overcome all others. In our time, the integrated combination of democratic institutions and industrial technology affords the best means to the fulfillment of men as persons. It permits, though it does not guarantee, progress towards human betterment. The United States is the vanguard and the leader. We have, therefore, all the duties of leadership in the march towards such achievement. Our unswerving commitment to that enterprise is the condition of successful leadership and power. It is also the price of preservation of our achievement and furtherance at home of our basic values. Our objective is therefore a leveling upward towards our own standards, political and economic. To that end we must confront and accept sacrifice. We must endure a slower progress at home than would be immediately but insecurely available on a more short-sighted and selfish basis.

In our striving towards common ends, we must make clear our awareness of the different and difficult conditions which other peoples confront. We must show that we accept the consequent limitations on their immediate achievement, even as we give them intelligent help towards a long-term betterment of their lot. At the same time, we must take all steps necessary to preserve our own economy and to maintain the creative drive of its established motivations. We must not give aid to others to the point of our own impoverishment and to the destruction of our own power. For instance, we must not, in making our home markets more readily available to others, bring major dislocations to our own communities. We must not by tariff reduction or removal destroy established industries or leave workers without employment. To weaken ourselves is to play into the hands of our opponents and to strengthen their power. An unrealistic benevolence which ruins or internally weakens our own economy as a going concern means long-term failure to achieve our professed purposes. It means decreased effectiveness in bringing about lasting improvements in the condition of others who seek our blessings and benefits. In the end, such a course gives victory without war to totalitarian Communism.

Such victory is Russia's immediate purpose. It is also its highest hope. Moreover, its achievement would give specious confirmation to Marxist-Leninist theory. Apart from Russian nationalistic ambitions, the policies of the Soviet Union are directed in fact and in intent to level others—the United States in particular—down towards its own very limited economic achievement. Through cold-war techniques, its dictatorship strives to make the combined burden of military aid and defense and economic assistance so great a strain on American resources as to destroy our effectiveness and undermine our power. Thereby it seeks to render plausible its claim that, quite apart from the selfishness of capitalists, the system of Western democracy and the public-welfare economy which rejects statist socialism are incapable of providing a basis for the betterment of other peoples. It strives to prove that our program of economic modernization and our technique for achieving a co-operative order of interdependent nations is unworkable where it is not hypocritical.

It behooves us, therefore, whatever the difficulties and strains, to demonstrate that the Soviet claims that our program is unworkable are as untrue as the Communist indictment that our whole intention is to exploit other peoples. For us to endeavor to protect and further our political and economic system and values at home without regard to others is to concede defeat in the bipolar struggle for the world. It is to prefer a precarious short-term well-being in an increasingly antagonistic world instead of the hard effort of leadership. To make such a choice is moral and spiritual self-corruption. Should we use the rules of private enterprise, of profit and loss, of sound investment and return, as criteria for giving or withholding aid to others, we shall likewise destroy ourselves, though more slowly. For such narrow and inappropriate calculations are emblematic of a failure of statesmanship. They reveal lack of awareness on the part of the policy-maker that, in the world today, gain and loss are political, not economic. And modern world politics rests ultimately on moral values and their ideological appeal.

Instruments and techniques: Bipartisanship, true and false

At the political level of party politics and the legislative way of life, Americans should reject the dogma and the misguidedly self-imposed constraint of bipartisan foreign policy. That policy has been much praised for its enlightened loyalty. Its reality has nevertheless sometimes been questioned. Bipartisanship has occasionally been indicted on grounds of partisan expediency. But the wisdom of the policy as practical political ethics is rarely challenged. Such a policy is no doubt requisite in times of collective emergency, of clear and present danger to the national whole. As intelligent and enlightened abstention from irresponsible partisanship, as loyal support of necessary financial and material means to implement particular policies at the moment in effect and not at once to be changed, it is also appropriate. Bipartisanship may likewise emerge and endure both in domestic and foreign affairs as an expression of a new consensus and the creation of a broad-based vital center. Then it is wholly admirable. For it constitutes the precondition to effective debate without danger of disruption. It provides the matrix for that continuity and coherence which gives a sense of security both to ourselves and others by permitting reasonably safe prediction of our future course. But beyond emergency, magnanimous loyalty, or genuine consensus, bipartisanship becomes a failure to transmit and transform the major elements which collectively constitute the interest of the social nation into a coherent, dynamically fluctuating, policy. It then involves abdication of a major brokerage function of the party system. It involves likewise an unwillingness or inability to offer constructive alternatives to existing policy within the framework of consensus. It thereby robs us of the democratic vitality of self-criticism and of a public opinion educated by controversy.

Happily, whatever the ceremonials of formal partisan voting, the total processes of legislation and of executive-legislative relations in this country are not such as to produce laws or policies which represent a strict majority view, and majoritarian attitude. The minority is not left utterly at loggerheads with the majority. It is not excluded from consideration in the making of law and policy. Consequently it does not outragedly reject *in toto* the actual decisions made. Moreover, American constitutionalism goes deeper than formal checks and balances, judicial review, or guaranteed rights. Indeed, conflicts in the United States are not fundamentally on party lines, and the English pattern of Government and Opposition is not our practice. For both parties represent a spectrum of opinion, and the centers of the two spectra constitute a majority and embody consensus. It would be unwise to abandon party planks, party alignments, and party debate in the realm of foreign, as of domestic, affairs. Rather, it is necessary to re-create debate within a range of agreement which transcends partisanship. Otherwise, we lose the advantage of dynamic and organic continuity in policy. We achieve at best a static and uncreative unity. We forego the confidence which comes from vital discussion. We sacrifice the enlightened national feeling to what is at root a statist line.

For the vital center is only vital when it is emergent from the interplay of diverse interests which voluntarily, and perhaps unconsciously, share an overriding common concern. Imposed as political duty, and by the eschewing of free debate, it is in fact devitalized and deleterious. Moreover, on the thesis here proclaimed that foreign and domestic policy are facets of one whole, partisanship in the one and bipartisanship in the other constitute on their face a ludicrous position, and one impossible long to maintain. If it could be maintained, moreover, it could be achieved only at the price of a pointless and harmful incoherence in total policy. That we today have a tendency to bipartisanship also in domestic affairs is in a sense true. For we are proceeding rapidly to eliminate or exclude as real influences extremists of right and left in both parties. But few would maintain that a lack of party issues within the new agreement is either desirable or probable. Certainly domestic bipartisanship is not a dogmatic duty. Moreover, a one-party state of two parties would on such terms be a serious threat to our democracy.

Bipartisanship may mean the following of administration policies by the minority party. It may also mean that curious brand of "me too-ism" on the part of the majority, of the executive, or of the relevant administrative departments under the executive, which has on occasion been evident in the endorsing and proclaiming of allegiance to minority doctrines of national interest and preachments of policy. In either event, it readily comes to constitute an internal appeasement which, in its lack of courage and conviction, can be more harmful than external appeasement. In the realm of policy, moreover, it begets an extreme oscillation between appeasement and aggressiveness in our dealings with other nations. Nor is this result accidental. In foreign affairs, bipartisanship developed out of crisis. It constitutes a superb democratic equivalent to emergency power and to dictatorship. But, the emergency past, it has encouraged emergency thinking and the conviction of insecurity, and has helped to make these unbalanced reactions a constant in our lives. Insofar as America has influence on world thinking, it has thereby contributed to the prolongation of emergency and to the failure to diminish international tensions. For, in the name of realism and loyalty, the artificial consensus of the bipartisan dogma has prevented that healthful enquiry and that ability to dissent without becoming suspect which help to generate realistic insight into the strength and limitations of opponents and the possible grounds of accommodation with them. Such bipartisanship helps to create and, once created, to strengthen stereotypes which inhibit thought and bring about violent emotion. Inevitably it becomes the handmaid of a dogma of utopian catastrophism, of that dangerous attitude which eschews moderate solutions by compromise and seeks a final and lasting, but humanly impossible, solution through a showdown. Such catastrophism is at least as inimical to effective policy as the utopianism of pure and practically undefiled moral aspiration. Both are equally satisfying as a substitute for that proper conduct of diplomacy which always necessitates the nerve of failure. A return to the normalcy of partisanship in all spheres of politics is a basic need for the effective pursuit of America's international interest. Such a return might also decrease the excessive compensatory strafing, despite our admitted range of agreement, over certain issues of domestic policy. By its very moderation, it would thereby aid in the creation of a truly vital center.

Instruments and techniques: Public participation in policy and propaganda

The representation and consultation of interested and informed groups is generally sound practice in the making and execution of public policies. Its value is no less great in foreign than in domestic affairs; and is in some ways even more valuable as insurance against merely governmental formulation of the national interest. The objective of such consideration of group viewpoints must be to render viable and to harmonize in a sustainedly coherent and dynamic pattern of policy the diverse elements which in their sum constitute the national interest of the American social order. Roughly what is needed is an equivalent, or a series of forces in their totality equivalent, to Calhoun's doctrine of concurrent majority, divorced from the sectional basis and the narrowed concept of interests of that suggestive teaching. Essentially the task is to intrude into the formulation and execution of day-by-day policy, with due regard to security considerations, the economic, social, and cultural interests which are essential parts of our political order.

Certain organizations which function in our domestic affairs, but came into existence and enjoy significance owing to our present world position and our resultant defense activities, may be relevant by loose but suggestive analogy. The local draft boards which operate our selective service system are the first and most obvious example. They are not composed of experts. They are bodies of ordinary citizens who agree to serve in their spare time and are chosen for the confidence they command locally. They express the sense and judgment of their communities. They work in the light of determined national needs and under general instructions and specific restraints. Different in structure and purpose, but also loosely relevant, were the War Labor Boards, national and regional, of the Second World War: and, despite all criticism, the Wage Stabilization Boards of more recent vintage. Their tripartite memberships brought into decision-making and policy-discussion representatives of the two interests, labor and industry, most specifically affected, and of the public at large.

In an area directly related to foreign policy, the State Department has a special section whose function it is to encourage and inform private organizations in states and cities devoted to the better understanding of UNESCO, and of America's role therein. Here, indeed, the relationship between officialdom and the public is different, and in form one-way. Moreover, the function itself is promotional and informational, rather than policy-making or administrative. Yet in practice such interchange tends to become one of mutual influence. Even though the purpose of the relationship may be to popularize official attitudes, the outcome is to aid expression of citizen views, and to further the conscious spread of concepts of the international interest of the national society. Again, while the widespread practice of using private experts as consultants on policy and as informants on foreign conditions is very different, in intention and in impact, from functional participation in administration, it tends towards similar consequences. The same also applies to the use of relevant private persons on the Voice of America program. In truth, we already possess, however rudimentary they be in form, and however inadequate in quantity, some of the practices and operational techniques most suited to procure and insure the dominance of a social, rather than a statist, concept of national interest. By the more widespread and effective use of such techniques and by proper reliance on public-spirited and competent citizens, we may insure that this social concept of national interest achieves internal recognition, and is accepted as the creative base of our international interest. We may thereby combat at the grass roots and in our daily conduct of affairs the narrower realism of American exclusiveness and superiority. Thereby, too, we can partially overcome internal controversies which arise from ignorance; and so do much to minimize needlessly harmful antagonism and distrust on the part of other peoples.

It is the part of wisdom, then, to broaden and systematize consultation and participation; to create a recognized and institutionalized citizen share in responsibility for policy; and to insure against bureaucratic perversion which renders the contributing citizen an enforced instrument of a statist line. Here again, conscious purpose on the part of participating citizens and clear awareness of the nature of American interest and of its relation to America's tradition and present role are the real insurances against a wrong orientation. They also prevent the reduction of the person to a servant of a putative interest he does not share, has not helped to make, and to which he may well become the sacrificial victim.

Curiously enough, a return to partisanship in our own international politics and a systematic development of consultation and participation in the development and execution of policy by those affected may actually aid, rather than hamper, the solution of one set of real problems which arises out of the modern conduct of diplomacy and the nature of modern publicity. In order to render diplomacy more effective, some moderates who are not at all enamored of the doctrine of amoral national interest nevertheless seek a return to the realism of the old European balance-of-power system. These critics have seen a connection between a moralizing utopianism which has often degenerated in practice into a "holier-than-thou" attitude on the part of America and the false democratization of politics through the appeal and organization of mass media of communication. Such media depend on lowest common denominator appeals. Necessarily, therefore, they enthrone the simplest moralities and indignations. Our diplomats are consequently subjected to irrelevant and uninformed criticism and to pressures which hamper rather than aid in the task of international bargaining and accommodation. In particular, the public work of international conferences suffers from premature publicity. In the event, the nation's international interest is harmed rather than helped.

Because the indictment is largely warranted, it is psychologically easy, especially for those who have a decent awareness of history, to contrast the present with the past. By a simple association, they relate secret diplomacy by trained diplomats, the balance-of-power system, and fairly stable peace achieved through unexciting adjustments made without publicity and without hurt prestige and lost face. They contrast such a climate of action with the present-day conduct of international relations, whether between individual nations or in the collective conferences of United Nations, under klieg lights. They deplore the constant tension, indignation, crisis, and conflict which are consequent on a necessity to be absolutely right. And indeed the techniques of an earlier diplomacy did have much to commend them. But the more recent search for open covenants openly arrived at rested precisely on the ground that commitments made in secret by an élite affected the fortunes and shaped the future of the whole body of citizens, whose interests were unconsulted. The system was in truth conducive to the political idea of national interest. It is peculiarly antithetical to the social concept of international interest. Yet that concept, slowly evolved and still new, is America's peculiar contribution by example to a better world order. What is more, as politics became democratized, while policy remained untouched by the peoples' hands, there developed that very dichotomy between internal and international affairs which it is necessary to overcome for the sake both of internal and international well-being.

A return to times past is no solution. Rather, it is necessary to determine the areas appropriate to the unobserved conduct of calm diplomacy by responsible statesmen. Then we must establish proper conditions and techniques for such work. But we must always make sure that the end product of their deliberations will be known, and subject to criticism. Moreover, wherever secrecy in the process of diplomacy may produce irremediable harm, regardless of the responsibility and responsiveness of statesmen, continuous public observation and discussion have to be assured.

The rightful area for open debate and for the general formation and expression of public opinion is the sphere of principle and over-all policy. Specific application, the dealing with individual situations and the ever-changing facts of never-static interests, is properly the region of that unwatched negotiation which permits give-and-take. For it necessitates something approaching arbitration, which cannot succeed without unembarrassed frankness in an atmosphere where imponderables and expediencies may be duly noted and assessed.

Our democracy, habituated to mass media of communication and to the ungentlemanly tactics which mark alike our politics and our national sport, too readily succumbs to the notion that all business which affects the public ought to be open to the public, regardless of its character or the sensibilities of other people. Yet to accept and follow that view results in a loss of the flexibility and accommodation so necessary to effective policy. On occasion, too, it leads to an absence of magnanimity and of respect for others which is little servicable to our own purposes as a world leader. Within our country, it may be noted, the ills which follow from indiscreet and uninformed publicity affect the proceedings of Congress as it deals with internal matters. Witness thereto is the daily publicity on congressional hearings and investigations. The consequence is often heat rather than light. Similar publicity on the meetings of Assembly and Security Council committees is certainly no less harmful.

In the realm of foreign affairs our diplomats, the relevant bureaucrats, and involved military personnel develop an understanding and an intelligent accommodatingness which is servicable to the nation's international interest. They have intimate familiarity and daily contact with representatives of other powers. While their conclusions and their policy recommendations need to be subjected to informed criticism, they must enjoy a certain latitude and protected privacy in their preliminary negotiations and routine operations. Moreover, dominant mass opinion is not an expression of the interest of the social nation, nor initially representative. It tends, rather, towards support of a power and statist line, at least under conditions where bipartisan policy initially leads towards a democratic totalitarian dogma rather than a genuine vital center.

Yet the danger involved in secret diplomacy is likewise a statist concept of national interest. For our national attitude is then in large part shaped by the élites responsible for the day-by-day conduct of foreign affairs. Unless checked, they normally develop a professional vested interest in certain policies, which they deem servicable to the nation. Possessed of intelligent understanding of other peoples and skill in dealing with them, they become convinced that their fellow citizens should view the national interest as what they themselves advocate. The relating of the layman to the processes of policy administration can create a very effective counterbalance and corrective to such dangerously well-meaning professional biases. For, provided his role is properly defined and implemented, he becomes an informed critic of the unpublicized conduct of detailed negotiations. He thereby constitutes a partial insurance against abuses, and helps prevent a too facile identification of public and professional interests. Simultaneously, he becomes a broker between government and public. He constitutes a source of enlightenment which can help diminish the naïve dogmas induced and sustained by mass media. Finally, the alert layman aids the politician in bridging the gap and diminishing the tension between misguided mass demands and responses which the latter dare not ignore, and enlightened assessment of our international interest, which is difficult enough even when he is free from such immediate pressures by his constituents.

VIII

Conclusion: America's mission

 ───────────────────────────────

However realistic our idealism, however idealistic our realism, the tasks of maintaining consequent policy, of generating and husbanding morally inspired power, of applying courageous and intelligent energy in a long-lived conflict of ways of and to life, will not be easy. By avoiding a narrowed realism we may prevent our loss of leadership and ultimate impotence through not becoming conspicuously irrelevant to the aspirations and needs of humanity at large. By avoiding utopianism and wishful thinking in our desire for peace in our time, we may escape being deluded by other's words and by self-deceit; we may eschew unprincipled concessions for the sake of peace but at the expense of law; and we may succeed in not confusing dangerous impotence with demonstrated integrity.

Then, however, though we achieve a real chance for meaningful and lasting success, we are driven to abandon hopes for instant and permanent solutions, and to accept the need for a sustained and coherent effort informed by a consistent objective, and maintained with determination at whatever price. That price may be high: we have to confront the possibility of Armageddon, wherein much of civilization might be destroyed.

For the conflict in our world is a basic one, wherein our opponent has wedded ancient national ambition to a crusading zeal on behalf of a perverted and perverse view of the process of human history and its destiny. From the alliance has come forth a corrupt but forceful tyranny which undevotedly exploits its parents in order to maintain and extend untrammeled and arbitrary power. We may expect calculatingness and ruthlessness from that tyranny: we cannot anticipate responsibility based on the acceptance of the central values of a rational and spiritual morality, which that tyranny, aided and supported by the ideology of materialism, incontinently rejects.

Anyone who has observed the twists and turns of the Communist party line must be aware that the official doctrine of any moment has little relevance to even Russia's own social and economic facts and needs: kulaks, and more recently Jews, are not the only classes sacrificed in the name of dogmas which, under the guise of continued class struggle, subversively subordinate and diminish the human resources and neglect the efficient exploitation for human welfare of the natural resources of the nation. But, for all the readiness of the rulers to sacrifice practicality and welfare to Marxist scripture and text, to deductions made from them, and to the outcome of preposterous debates among captive schoolmen, it would be erroneous to infer that we confront a deductive rational system at once rigorous and ruthless. For the dominant tyrant of the moment has no scruple over changing the meaning of texts and the content of appropriate deductions to suit his purposes, whether to warrant liquidation of real or putative rivals at home, to justify changes in direction or tempo of internal policies, or to create propaganda abroad serviceable to calculations of what for the moment most promises advantage.

Nor have we any good grounds for believing that change is in the offing; that the basic techniques of Soviet dictatorship will be voluntarily modified or abandoned through internal pressures; that struggles for control among the ruling party group will lead to its collapse, to civil war, or to revolution; that popular discontents will prove directly explosive and fatal to the rulers; that opposition can be readily organized; that a combination of internal prosperity and manifest collective power will lead to a concern for public welfare and personal freedom; or that the rulers of the U.S.S.R. will change their minds as to the nature and prospects, moral and material, of the West, with consequent changes in policy. Both the Soviet dictatorship and the Soviet practice of international relations, so largely based on its needs, fears, and hopes, seem well established. They are apt to continue unless ambition, felt insecurity, or the need to exploit supposed evils elsewhere for morale and public organization at home lead to aggressive war and to defeat in it; or until over a long period external action and inner discontent promote conditions for, and a will to, effective revolution without war.

In Russia, internal struggles for power, with periodic liquidations of former leaders and their supporters, will in all probability recur. They are, indeed, an inescapable necessity of personal dictatorship in the Soviet one-party state; and a valuable technique simultaneously to avoid sustained dissension and overcome competition at the top, to engender fear and submissiveness, and to distract attention from failures to pursue or achieve the professed ideals by means of blaming scapegoats, who are dubbed class enemies. Such struggles are not, however, a sign of weakness. They do not betoken a régime on the verge of collapse. They do not warrant hopes for the easy promotion of successful revolution. Trials of leaders, liquidations, and changes in party line may all provide us with effective bases for propaganda to undecided peoples. They also reveal the essential nature of the régime and give us periodic reminders of the folly of naïve optimism and misguided good will.

By the same token, they warn us that a régime which uses such techniques is unlikely to bring to the top men of international good will, undogmatic accommodatingness, and a desire to implement at home the democratic promise of freedom on a basis of equality which is the high ideal of theoretical communism. Psychologically and sociologically, means and ends are interdependent, and methods shape results. The techniques of rule, and of struggle for rulership, at present prevalent in the Soviet Union, and there firmly established as pragmatically successful, are unlikely to bring to the fore the personality types who desire to create, or could function effectively in, a free democratic order. Nor are successful leaders there apt to be men tolerant of the Western way, or by temperament or interest comprehendingly sympathetic to it. Genuine collaboration is no more to be expected than immediate internal collapse.

Rather, the Russian leaders, from conviction and as a technique of sustained power and supporting morale at home, may be expected to seek continuously and to await expectantly our own collapse: they will design their own policy, internal and international, both to make their wish come true and to take advantage of ills in our system when they occur.

In such a course, their system has certain short-term advantages based on a specious coherence. The neat harnessing of the universalist ethic of utopian Marxism to the exclusive and particularist imperial ambition of Russia by dictators who exploit both, in order to attain security in power, gives seeming warrant to totalitarianism, to militarism, and to a rigid Iron Curtain. For the rationale of the system, the greatest hoax in modern history, is that Russia as a communist society is the leader and special guardian of the ideal communist ethic in a generally hostile world. It therefore has a right to demand undeviating allegiance and submission from the friends of justice, liberty, and equality everywhere, regardless of supposed duty to their own nations, whose governments are oppressive enemies of virtue. It has a right to demand of its own people absolute obedience and ardent acceptance of imposed sacrifices and privations for the sake of humanity elsewhere, and for the human future. It has an obligation to protect them and their leaders from contamination from without, which takes subtle as well as obvious forms: non-Communist countries are a new Calvinist devil forever at work to corrupt the worshippers at the Marxist shrine. It has a duty to use every resource to protect its safety, territorial, institutional, and ideological, and to ready itself for others' deliverance, purification, and orthodox organization when the time is ripe.

As a consequence of such a rationale, the Russian economy may properly be devoted, as it is devoted, to the creation of an effective military machine. Transport and industry have as their prime function direct or indirect service to the arsenal of the professed champion of world communism; and, since all Russia's citizens are themselves conceived as devoted instruments of that end, which is synonymous with Russia's own greatness and expansion, they too become economic tools and military weapons, whose wants are to be considered and met only to the point needful for their efficiency and morale as instruments. In this sense, propaganda and brutal force which inspires fear are likewise parts of the productive economy: they too help to create and maintain a military machine usable on behalf of the overall policy, the current line, and the ruling dictators.

This coherent ideology in action throughout the economy does not simply forge a powerful military weapon: it is itself a powerful political-economic weapon in a cold war which on Russian Communist doctrine is inevitable, and must continue unabated until, with or without the supplement of hot or shooting war, the "cause" has achieved global triumph. That cause not only permits, but positively warrants, the treatment both of Russia's vast area and population and of all allied countries as a Spartan armed camp: totalitarian military discipline, including a necessary military police, summary justice, and terrorism against those found to be class opponents, is moral virtue, not evil: it is designed for the security of an order which is the instrument of ultimate human liberation and dignity. But such organization creates a nice efficiency in the use of scarce means, of limited productive capacity and technology and of still inadequate skills, which in combination would not at present permit free competition—or comparison, on the basis of consumer welfare—with the Western, and particularly the American, achievement. The doctrine, then, either avoids or warrants suppression of discontent at home. By monomaniacal devotion to a single and sinister purpose it allows the building of a military machine that compares favorably with the West, which it threatens. Apart from resources, labor, and technical skills, it utilizes and directs the work of scientific research with similar economy, and thereby again equalizes competition with the West, where its purposes are more diverse and its practitioners largely free. The Iron Curtain, by hiding from the Russian people the content of Western professions and Western respect for fact, and their contrast with Soviet pronouncements in United Nations, facilitates maintenance of the thesis that our intentions are hostilely imperialistic, and that the U.S.S.R. is the bulwark of democratic freedom for nonindustrialized peoples. It likewise allows the Russian people to be persuaded variously that our economic advantages are temporary; that they are nonexistent, and our standards inferior; and that our system is in slow decline, or on the verge of crisis and catastrophe which will engulf us, and bring about the overthrow of our so-called democratic régime, at any moment. Meanwhile, the Russian leaders can with impunity claim priority in all modern inventions, monopoly of scientific understanding and achievement, and superior culture and dissemination of culture.

The arsenal of Soviet Communism and the Iron Curtain thereby work hand in hand as both a coherent internal policy and an international weapon of cold war designed by its very maintenance to provoke and promote in the West the attitudes and the conditions respectively complained of and prophesied. The disrespect for fact, the intransigent hostility, the dogmatic aggressiveness, and the calculated encouragement of disloyalty and subversion which mark the behavior of the Russian leaders do indeed produce resistance, defense, and internal self-defense in the West. These measures are further supported and encouraged by a decent moral resentment at the oppressive character of the Russian dictatorship over its own people and its satellites. That angry concern is, however, usefully represented by the party-leaders to the Russian people as hostility to them, and a desire to intervene and overthrow their superior system; even though the Russian rulers may also, as a convenient tactic in international affairs, endorse legal or ethical doctrines of nonintervention, and encourage their advocates.

Meanwhile, the Russian sacrifice of all other considerations to armament forces the West, particularly this country, to devote much of its budget to defense. But we are committed to continuous and progessive social welfare here-now, and neither would nor could anyone persuade the American people or its allies that all must be sacrificed to an indefinite future whose realization is threatened by a dog-in-the-manger enemy. Consequently the strains on our resources and the threats of repeated dislocations of the economy as we readjust under changing circumstances to meet both needs are in truth very great. Nor are they diminished by the pressures, on the one hand, of moralists and self-interested citizens who, desiring less taxes, clamor for decreased armaments, and, on the other, by equally self-interested groups who, fearing the impact of decreased government contracts and spreading that fear abroad among us, help to create a psychology of crisis and dislocation and to diminish our chances of smooth adjustments.

Under a specious guise of national- and world-communist welfare, the Soviet leaders avoid that relaxing of continuous emergency government which would be thrust upon them with a reorientation towards peace and internal prosperity. Such a tactic actually tends to reduce the higher living standards of the West towards the Russian level. It also creates difficulties of adjustment which, in the absence of high statesmanship and citizen good sense, might lead to that depression and crisis which the Soviet rulers so eagerly desire and so pantingly await.

For in truth the whole Russian policy, designed to insure the safety of tyranny at home by the Machiavellian tactic of creating, maintaining, and combatting enemies abroad, is a deliberate dog-in-the-manger attitude. The Party élite, aware of the long gap between Russia's standard of living in the foreseeable future and the Western achievement, actually prevents Russian betterment to preserve its own status and supposedly necessary function. It too relies on that most dangerously pervasive of social generalizations, Gresham's Law, deliberately yet needlessly casting itself in the role of bad money, attempting to drive out the good coin of the West. It hopes through its consequent strategy in support of antiquated Marxist dogma to bring off the *coup* of the greatest of all self-fulfilling prophecies.

The task of the West, and especially of the United States as Western leader, is to prevent fulfillment of that prophecy. It must show its capacity, by the countervailing social power of democratic institutions and coherent policies, to circumvent the deleterious operation of that social Gresham's Law. By demonstration of calmly ardent commitment to the realization of a rational ethic of personality through free social institutions at home and abroad, it must make clear both the superiority and the universal availability of the antitotalitarian and pro-human way. That whole task necessitates sustained attention and devotion, in thought and action, at many levels and in many directions.

In our attitudes to, and dealings with, Russia, its peoples, and its satellite populations, we need to overcome confusion. We have tended to believe variously that the Russian people, being unaccustomed to self-government, were appropriately ruled by the present dictatorship; that they were loyal to it, so that propaganda against it was futile, all the difficulties of the Iron Curtain apart; and, quite contradictorily, that they groaned under oppression, awaiting deliverance, and would revolt at once and successfully were it not for the horde of secret police, informers, and agents-provocateurs who, themselves uneasy yet enmeshed, made life a horror of insecurity, and nights a prolonged nightmare. We have thus posed to ourselves curious alternatives: either, as a matter of national self-interest, we must combat the ambitions of the Russian rulers and people abroad, but must acknowledge the former's right to be tyrannical within, and must not aim at, or hope for, a radically different régime, before or after war; or we could readily gain the support of the victims of tyranny, who long to throw off their chains, would do so given proper aid, and would then forthwith become modern Western democrats.

On grounds of common sense and a minimal knowledge of social psychology and modern history, these alternatives are patently absurd. No people, no normal persons, Eastern or Western, ancient or modern, delight in death and the fear of death; enjoy haunted sleep; welcome broken families; get pleasure from apprehension of torture to their bodies; and luxuriate in the constant discipline of suppressed thoughts and uncertainties as to the consequences of expressed ones. Yet that these conditions are the regular circumstances of Russian life, all too ample evidence attests. Reactions to them no doubt range the gamut from a harried apprehensiveness and the strain of imaginings cumulatively worse than any possible event, through dull exhaustion and apathy, to a sturdy pursuit of daily tasks in a situation where imminent danger is the habitual setting of life. No doubt, too, some persons may achieve an outwardly gay insouciance, or develop the gambler's fixed impassivity. Yet most Russians, aside from some (but not all) of the beneficiaries of the régime, like any other people under similar conditions, would prefer deliverance from such evils were they to see a means and a meaningful alternative, and were the costs not impossibly high. The need for purges; government appeals for loyalty; attested reports of constant inefficiencies, corruption, and sabotage —these all suggest that discontents and frustrations will out, even though the protests be futile, and even though they beget greater repression than before.

The distance between such behavior and effective organization for the conduct of revolution is, however, enormous, as Lenin's own searching analysis of the requirements for the latter should long since have made us aware. What is more, national loyalty is in our time among men's first loyalties, and its intensity is not diminished either by a relatively new sense of Russian national power and prestige, or by the conviction, however induced, and whether true or false, of hostility on the part of other nations or blocs. Hence resentment against internal dictatorship, or, better, against its impact on men's fear-ridden daily lives, is offset by national loyalty, by fears of other powers, and by the lack of alternative leadership for defense. It is, indeed, readily distracted from its proper objects and safely canalized into organized hatred of the West. Men may loathe their rulers, be conscious of tyranny, and take exasperated action in self-defense or to express resentment without the hope of establishing a better order through revolution; and even with a sure conviction that any such undertaking would aid a greater, because alien, enemy, and would bring worse disaster.

Such ambivalence is precisely the setting of our task in endeavoring to combat the Russian tyranny and gain support from within the country. It constitutes the difficult condition of appeals beamed behind the Iron Curtain. It is folly for us to take a strict noninterventionist position, on the ground that Russia's affairs are her own, and that her people, at one with their rulers, are incapable of instituting, operating, or enjoying any sort of freer institutions. To do so is to reject from the outset the view that the ethics of personality and democracy has any universal validity, and to espouse an absolute relativism. Such a position will not help us in dealing with Russia. It will not allow us to persuade its people that their own rulers are wrong in claiming that we are hostile to the Russian people and their national integrity. Rather, we shall simply have facilitated maintenance of the Iron Curtain, and misrepresentation behind it. Likewise, we shall have abandoned any possibility of giving hope or leadership to satellite peoples where these are in fact captive and resentful. We shall have lost the battle for undecided peoples who, though persuaded that we are not imperialist or opposed to their national aspirations, will also conclude that we offer no alternative to the Soviet promise of a better world and life. Above all, we shall have lost our own sense of leadership in defense of great values, grounded in tradition and demonstrated by reason. The final consequence could well be abandonment of our convinced maintenance of free institutions at home.

Yet to seek the showdown of war against Russia on our own terms and in our own time, a course sometimes advocated on grounds of strategy and of a conviction of war's inevitability, would be equally misguided. Indeed, the appeal of such a program rests mainly on nerves, on our desire to escape sustained tension and cut the Gordian knot. In truth, the most difficult condition of effective Western, and in particular American, policy, is the need lastingly to confront and bear such strain and to maintain level-headedness in the process. For, all the destructive horror of atomic warfare apart, our own victory in such an endeavor so undertaken would not be triumph for the cause of democratic freedom as a universal morality. We should then indeed appear the enemy, not simply of the Communist dogma, or of its further perversion and abuse by dictator and Party leadership, but of the Russian people and nation. Though the existing régime fell in defeat, the dual task of creating free institutions without threat of totalitarian revivals through patriotic appeal, and of furthering the reign of peaceful world law grounded in principles of common humanity would be hampered, and indefinitely delayed.

Our own strategy, which may indeed lead soon or late to war being thrust upon us by an increasingly insecure Russian régime, must be directed to encouraging germs of discontent within the Soviet Union and its satellites wherever possible, and to the extent possible. We must organize and aid potential revolutionaries there, yet as far as possible restrain them from ill-calculated or premature action. We must persuade the Russian people that we are opposed to a tyranny which at once deprives them of immediately available material well-being, personal security, and freedom, and threatens the peace and prospects of ameliorative prosperity for the rest of the world. We must ourselves develop our own system, including its military power, so that at the ripe moment we may aid them first to throw off their chains with minimum cost and disruption, and then to reconstruct society on their own design and tradition, without undue suffering, and without intervention designed to impose our special dogmas or institutions or to further interests peculiar to ourselves.

Such a program may seem to involve fighting fire with fire, normally a dubious proposition from the moral viewpoint. Certainly it necessitates encouragement of subversion and disloyalty to the Russian government. Yet such tactics, used to harm our institutions, are one of our basic complaints against Russian-sponsored international Communism, and the ground, until recently, for our present attitudes toward American Communists and the Communist party. Hence, to advocate such a course on our part may appear to involve mere bias, to make our principles relative to whose ox is gored, to reject the dictate of disinterested reason that sauce for the goose is sauce for the gander, and so to put ourselves on a par with our opponents and lose all chance of persuading hesitant peoples of the superior ethical claims of our own social philosophy in action.

In form, indeed, such an indictment is correct. Nevertheless, though imperfect man may never achieve his ideals completely, and may not even formulate them with absolute and final correctness, warrant is not thereby given for a complete relativism. Strategies gain validation, not simply from appropriateness to purpose, but from the soundness of the purpose itself. The overall thesis here propounded is that the present bipolar conflict involves a fundamental issue between ways of life and concepts of man, not a mere struggle between powers which share a common view of life and its values, but have different interests and inevitably distorting vantage points. Further, while Communist doctrine claims universal validity, the Soviet government is a totalitarian tyranny which oppresses its own people, reduced to mere means on behalf of ends beyond, and exclusive of, themselves. Likewise, it is particularist in that its only concept of universal duty is a like submission by all others to itself. Not less than Nazism, though less frankly, and indeed with a specious contrary profession, it rejects both that common humanity which rests on the ultimacy of persons and that tolerance of institutional diversity which, given men's special circumstances and traditions and their resultant common though differing limitations, is its proper corollary. Its encouragement of subversion elsewhere and its oppression at home are thus both alike attacks on man's meaning. To attempt to subvert it and to combat its infiltration in the name and by the means of a theory and practice of life which, in rejecting its claims as at best moral error and at most a rationalization of self-conscious immorality, themselves assert both the universal rights of persons and their particular local needs as conditions for effective pursuit and realization of those rights, is therefore a moral imperative. In this sense, the end justifies the use of necessary means in the one case, as it warrants condemning their employment, by reason of condemning their purpose, in the other. If the end is good, the *appropriate* means are indeed permitted. Moreover, their employment is then an obligation. But an evil end makes means thereto evil in proportion to their appropriateness to its achievement.

The above assertions, however, re-emphasize the nature and dimensions of our task, which is indeed meaningless or futile if men anywhere genuinely desire and love tyranny and regard themselves and their lives as without value or meaning. Likewise, the interpretation here given is erroneous and dangerously misleading if the Russian leadership is morally principled, nonarbitrary, and constitutionally subject to the rule of law at home; and if it respects persons and the diversities of peoples and their institutions abroad. But if it does not, then (to reiterate for emphasis) we must at once insist that it does not. We must make clear its falsity and its moral failure to those deluded by its rationalizations and not convinced otherwise by direct experience or knowledge. We must show convincingly that we, on the contrary, do follow our professed respect for men and peoples, alike in our society at home, in our present dealings with allies and hesitant neutrals, in our immediate program for relations respectively with the Russian government and the Russian people, and in our plans for lasting assistance to the latter that they may achieve and shape their own free institutions.

This needful attitude and policy towards the Soviet bloc and its component nations, who are in one sense the most urgent of our concerns and in another constitute the locus of a last battle in our struggle for a reign of international law, a comity of peoples, and the world-wide prevalence of humanistic principle, is simply the expression at a critical point of the whole policy to whose exploration and defense the preceding pages have been devoted. That policy rests on our moral heritage and our social and political institutions, whose furtherance and protection are not only conditions of our inner security and spiritual welfare at home, but also the very grounds of any legitimate claim to leadership in and for a free world of liberated persons.

To perform our role effectively and preserve our society as a moral venture we need clarity as to their nature and commitment to the values implicit or explicit in them. Such clarity constitutes our generative drive towards the creative release and direction of individual and social energies. For only by positive commitment can we combat and overcome tendencies to insecurity and lostness and thereby achieve not simply the nerve of failure, easy in crisis yet dangerous, but the more important and difficult nerve of imperfect success and constant striving. We must be calmly aware that utopia never comes, and we must cease to want or expect it. Such an attitude is necessary to avoid a sense of futility and of functionlessness, and to escape those collective psychic miseries whereby the groundwork is laid for dictatorship as supposed deliverance and the restoration of apparent purpose in life. Such moral armament is our lasting and impregnable defense against that social and personal insecurity which is far more profoundly subversive alike of our institutions and of the value-system we share with others than any misguided band of Communists boring from within, however sinister the latter be, and however vital it is to combat them. For, once given a clear social philosophy and purpose, we can transform recurrent crises and nervous tensions into the security of sustainedly purposeful striving. Threats then become purely external, the consequence of the uncertain actions of our polar enemy. But then such threats can be squarely confronted, and the variables for prediction and policy are greatly decreased, since our own position is clear. The very dangers then strengthen, rather than weaken, our unswerving course.

Yet the nature of our heritage; of America's institutional embodiment and furtherance of it; of the present promise in our way of life and our achievements for its preservation and development in the future; and of the necessary affirmations and rejections to insure such development and avoid corruption—these are all in their essentials clear and simple.

Our central heritage is, first, the Graeco-Roman concept of man the social-political animal and of law as restraining and enabling principle for his realization. Secondly, it comprises the Hebraic-Christian revelation of man the essential person, endowed with ultimate dignity and worth, and never to be fully cabined and confined in the matrix of earthly institutions, which are his necessary servants but never his final and all-inclusive masters. For centuries the Western world has struggled to realize these insights, ultimately compatible and mutually sustaining, yet often in seeming conflict, whether through falsely extreme formulations or through the inadequacies of human knowledge and powers of control over men and environments, over difference and distance.

Much of European history is concerned with the search for an operable and efficient order of law; with the achievement of a national system which would overcome localism, secure citizens against private violence, and create collective power and prosperity. In the course of that effort, freedom of the person was generally held of minor moment: the evocation of common loyalty to the nation and its ruler was the prerequisite and foundation of secure order. Success in the endeavor brought absolute monarchy, mercantilist regulation, and the doctrine of state sovereignty.

These in due course proved frustrating, and became corrupted, in forgetfulness of initial purpose and achievement. Men then sought to constitutionalize power, to participate in its control or exercise, to gain freedoms for worship, thought, and enterprise. In the struggles which began with the English Civil War, continued through the Glorious Revolution and the French Revolution, and filled the nineteenth century with reforms and revolts designed in the main to achieve representative and responsible parliamentary government, the overall objectives were attained throughout a large area of Europe, and, prior to the Revolution of 1917, seemed on the way to attainment even in Russia.

Nevertheless, these achievements occurred within the pattern of the sovereign nation-state and of settled hierarchical societies. Sovereignty was transferred; national loyalty was transformed and strengthened as popular identification with the nation and its public power and prestige. The state, even when it was not master, remained the master-symbol; and life came to have a dominantly political focus, whose outcome was potentially statist. Rights were conditional, save where, as in England, they had become traditional; and majorities tended to enjoy the once unchallenged claims of absolute monarchs. Thus the full reconciliation in a free and varied society of the two great elements in the Western tradition remained imperfectly realized, and the Christian dignity of the person was always imperfectly secure in the face of the state, potentially even when not actually men's master. And, as should now be clear, Marxist Communism, for all its ethical inspiration, and in the face of its own professed enmity to the state, ended by exaggerating the statist element in Europe's development, and in the name of human liberation produced a totalitarian tyranny which laughed at the whole idea of personal rights and ruthlessly sacrificed persons.

By contrast with Europe, America, aided by a virgin continent ripe for settlement and rich in unused, and largely unoccupied, resources, pursued a different course which promised to harmonize the values of Western man and to a considerable degree brought realization of the promise. From Colonial days many of our English settlers were critical of, or hostile to, monarchical pretensions. Ardent in their Protestantism, they were fully aware of the limitations of the political view of life and of the inadequacy to the good life of an all-embracing public order. Later, our federal constitutional system, with all its intricate checks and balances and its rejection of a single and centralized sovereignty, provided the organization for a political system which itself militated against statism; while the Bill of Rights insured against total reduction of the person to a subject citizen.

Our long-lived frontier and the vast reach of a subcontinent provided further security against governmental control and development of the nation, without preventing use of government as a convenient instrumentality and support in the furtherance of men's diverse independent enterprises. But the roots of our undertakings were the self-helping individual and the voluntary co-operating group. Subsequently, with much travail, we assured indeed that a national loyalty and pride, which yet were not our sole or always dominant attachments even in the political realm, should be reflected in a due and secure unity. Yet the many from which the one was made were not lost or swallowed in the process. Sectional and local loyalties and numerous governments which supplied services attached to themselves interests; and sustained citizen interest remained. Likewise, our social order continued to be pluralistic. The sense and accomplishment of Greek citizenship as a full participation in all the activities of life here resulted from the interplay of private, semipublic, and public and official groups at all levels of life and on every scale, local, state, regional, and national. The federal government itself came to fill the dual role of participating partner and overall protector of this adventure in social living. We always were, in time more conspicuously became, and today remain, a social rather than a narrowly political nation, whose highest loyalty and commitment is to the American way of life rather than simply or exclusively to the United States government.

In such an order, personal rights have indeed enjoyed the protection of institutional freedom, of escape from abridgement by very reason of the variety of our authorities and of the support given them, often from ulterior motives, by other interests. Yet they have also remained secure and healthy by very reason of our activist release of energies: by their constant exercise in a society where the presumption is in favor of joining and of causes, and not of initiation of new undertakings by government, or of waiting for the action of a recognized élite.

What is more, for all the past abuses and continuing defects in our economic and industrial order, the development of American resources to the point of our present technological pre-eminence has at once been aided by and has enrichingly complemented the ethos of political federalism and social pluralism. Conjointly with them, it has progressively made available to more and more of our inhabitants adequate material means for their independence and security, so that all may be effective democratic citizens, unhampered by the short-sightedness which comes from urgent want, debasing toil, and an uncertain tomorrow. Likewise, it now makes leisure and pleasure the normal lot, and so opens the way to cultural and spiritual fulfillment of diverse personalities in that area of final goods where, granted a decent tolerance, varied satisfactions need not conflict, but can enrich at once the individual and the social order.

In short, by reason of our institutions, and aided by our environmental fortune, we have progressively achieved a rich society whose material triumphs do not portend a vulgar materialism, but promote and make possible for most men and women, and in ideal for all, the creative release of their energies and the realization of their personalities. We are fortified by the reaches and riches and the generative power of a subcontinental nation. We are served alike by industrial technology and governments as co-operative instruments for a public-welfare society. We are intensely committed to group action for public not less than private purposes. Our common allegiance rests on, and is reinforced by, institutional insurance and furtherance of political and social liberties and participation, and freedom for individual preferences and pursuits. By heritage and practice we constitute the middle-class classless society of free persons.

That achievement, and its continued insurance and furtherance, is the just basis of our claim to principled leadership in the world. It comprises our answer to Soviet Communism, and it offers a superior alternative to others who will emulate our way and seek and enjoy our help. The chapters of this book have been devoted to showing the implications for foreign policy of that way. They have attempted to combat those erroneous ideas which, in our day of power and leadership, would lead us in supreme folly back to a European pattern; even though Europe, through inescapable heritage and despite ardent efforts, could not adequately realize, as we through fortune and energy may realize, the shared insights of Western culture. Yet the universality and rationality of Western values make them the common aspiration of all peoples.

But the implication of the preceding argument is that policy for our leadership in and for a free, because morally and institutionally liberated, world, must rest on clarified commitment to the strengthening and further realization of our central insights and best institutional practice at home. Such achievement necessitates uncompromising support of the method of freedom, of a constitutional democracy engined by a free politics which accepts men's finiteness and uncertainty, and cherishes rights as conditions imposed by that uncertainty and as means to utilize human resources and release human energies to the maximum degree possible compatibly with such support. We need, therefore, to overcome the continuing blemishes in our society and to extend the reach of rights. Aware of the need for stability and gradualness, and of the claims of vested as well as unvested interests, we must then acknowledge with a sense of proportion those real social ills and injustices, whether they affect Negroes or Indians, slum-dwellers or tenant farmers, on which Communists excessively harp. And we must progressively correct them and seek to equalize the range of choices open to men, as we have so long and successfully been doing, despite hesitancies and resistances.

By the same token, we must forthrightly insist that our method of freedom is the way of self-correctingness by men who, while courageously committed to the truth that man is valuable and a moral animal, possess no final truth. We are lastingly seekers for enlightenment, proceeding from the knowledge and with the resources we have into an uncertain future which is yet by our method to be made as enriching, and rendered as little dangerous, as human powers permit. Then, however, for the very sake of that creative venturing, we must refuse to acknowledge any right to use our freedoms for the avowed purpose of sabotaging or subverting them by guile and force. Claimed rights to that end must be denied; and we must, where need be, revamp ancient protections against arbitrary monarchs so as to secure our society, and those governmental institutions which are its valued servants and supports, against enemies internal as well as external. We must abandon the incubus of a dogmatic liberalism that is falsely tolerant; and we must avoid that heresy-hunting which, ardent to preserve us against the consequences of false tolerance, threatens also the right and claim to proper diversity and dissidence.

In so doing, we take out potent insurance, by our clear consensus and consequent collaboration, against needless occurrence of those crises and conflicts which the Soviet leaders have so long insisted are inevitable in capitalist democracy, have so impatiently awaited, and have sought to bring about in order to exploit. Likewise, to the rest of the world we thereby can give assurance at once of our stability and of our clear vision. Then we can hope for their commitment to our cause without reservation, since they will be assured that we are committed and consequent, and will not fear either that we will retire into our shell in the time of their troubles or will fish in muddied waters in hopes of an unexpected haul at their expense.

On such a foundation we may adopt, and more nobly adapt, the Roman concept of mission in the world:

Tu regere imperio populos, Romane, memento
Hae tibi erunt artes, pacisque imponere morem,
Parcere subiectis, et debellare superbos.

(Virgil, Aeneid VI, 851-53)

But, Rome, 'tis thine alone, with awful sway,
To rule mankind, and make the world obey,
Disposing peace and war by thy own majestic way;
To tame the proud, the fetter'd slave to free:
These are imperial arts, and worthy thee.

(Dryden translation)

For our sway over others will be no imperial rule, but the respected influence of demonstrated success and primacy in devotion to a common humanity. Our arts will be wise assistance and unfailing support towards liberation, towards others sharing in and contributing to a common, yet vastly rich and varied, culture. Peace will indeed be our end, and a custom sought for the world, through international law and international institutions founded on principle, to which we ourselves are also willingly subject because their leading proponents. In search of that law, it will be our ardent mission not simply to spare the humble but to deliver the oppressed. To that end we shall indeed make war *à outrance*, with no compromise, on the proud dictators who pervert all principle and debase men whom they have first oppressed. Thus our moral empire will rest on a freely accepted appeal to the minds and hearts of peoples liberated with our assistance, enjoying our respect on grounds of a common humanity, and welcomed as partners in the human venture who by their efforts and insights enrich the stock of human culture. Only such uncompulsive empire is consonant with our heritage, our insights, our concept of mission, and the moral security of our own institutions. By reason of that heritage and inspiration, we can accept no less, and seek no more.

Index